THE BOOK OF
POTENTIALLY
CATASTROPHIC
SCIENCE

by Sean Connolly

WORKMAN PUBLISHING
NEW YORK

Library of Congress Cataloging-in-Publication Data is available.

ISBN 978-0-7611-5687-1

Workman books are available at special discounts when purchased in bulk for premiums and sales promotions as well as for fund-raising or educational use. Special editions or book excerpts also can be created to specification. For details, contact the Special Sales Director at the address below.

Cover design by Raquel Jaramillo
Cover illustration by Lou Brooks
Design by Netta Rabin
Illustrations by Robert James

Photo credits: **Alamy:** Arco Images GmbH p. 293; Bildagentur-online/McPhoto p. xiv tool, p. 4, p. 5, p. 88; Tibor Bognar p. xiv background; Classic Image p. 131; ClassicStock p. 193; Simon Hadley p. 298; Mark Hamilton p. 227; Interfoto p. v bottom, p. vii bottom, p. x, p. 34, p. 63, p. 69, p. 71, p. 172, p. 190, p. 198; The London Archive p. 81; The London Art Archive p. 20; Lordprice Collection p. 174; Mary Evans Picture Library p. 24, p. 60, p. 64, p. 111, p. 121, p. 164, p. 244 left, p. 244 right, p. 250, p. 156 right; The Natural History Museum p. vii top, p. 154 men; North Wind Picture Archive p. iv bottom, p. 8, p. 16, p. 91 bottom, p. 144; Colin Palmer Photography p. 291; Photo Researchers p. 200, p. 203; Photos 12 p. 98; Pictorial Press Ltd. p. 108, p. 260; Paris Pierce p. viii bottom, p 253; The Print Collector p. vi, p. 26, p. 27; Robert Harding Picture Library Ltd. p. 18, p. 19; Alistair Scott p. 300–301; StockShot p. 288; Universal Images Group Ltd. p. xiv Homo Erectus; Rob Walls p. 55; World History Archive p. vii middle, p. 78, p. 91 top, p. 101, p. 146, p. 162, p. 216; p. 254. **Boneclones.com:** p. 10. **Bridgeman Art Library:** The Heart/Gautier D'Agoty/Arnauld Eloi (1741–1780/83)/Musée d'Histoire de la Médecine, Paris, France/Archives Charmet p. ix, p. 278. **Fotolia:** p. 2 top, p. 3, p. 37, p. 48, p. 52 background, p. 54, p. 70, p. 118, p. 147, p. 157, p. 165, p. 183, p. 195, p. 245, p. 246, p. 272, p. 290. **Getty Images:** p. 206, p. 209, p. 218, p. 232, p. 281; De Agostini p. iv top, p. 2; Popperfoto p. 180; SSPL p. v top, p. 44, p. 47; Time & Life Pictures p. 224, p. 234, p. 235, p. 270. **iStockphoto:** p. viii top, cover mushroom cloud, p. 242, p. 247. **Library of Congress:** p. vi, p. 68, p. 130, p. 128, p. 139, p. 156 left.

Workman Publishing Company, Inc.
225 Varick Street
New York, NY 10014-4381
workman.com

Printed in the United States of America

First printing March 2010
10 9 8 7 6 5 4 3

To Frederika, for showing me my potential—
and helping to avert catastrophes

I am indebted to Raquel Jaramillo at Workman for her enthusiasm
and vision at every stage of the writing and production of this book.
In addition, I would like to thank the following individuals
and organizations for their help and inspiration:

Frank Ciccotti, James Dalton, Benjamin Joyce, Dr. Jeff Kenna,
Dr. Peter Lydon, William Matthiesen, Dr. Sarah Morse,
Professor Jay Pasachoff, Oliver Pugh, Peter Rielly, Elizabeth Stell,
Bath Literature Festival, Berkshire Film and Video, Camco International,
Hostelling International, Leabharlann Contae Chiarrai, University of Oxford,
Williams College, and Woods Hole Oceanographic Institution.

CONTENTS

INTRODUCTION

Hey—just why is it that scientists so often get that pesky adjective "mad" tacked on to their job description? After all, they work hard studying the world and how it works and then develop new ideas, test them, and share their knowledge with the rest of us. And before you know it, we wind up with fire to cook with, the wheel to help transport us places, telescopes to let us view the far reaches of the galaxy, and even X-ray machines to see the invisible rays our eyes alone can't see. What's so crazy about all that?

Maybe this "mad" idea has nothing to do with the scientists, but more to do with the rest of us. After all, it's the public (rather than the scientists) who usually considers it mad to send a ship sailing over the edge of a cliff, or to jump out of a balloon with only a few yards of silk to slow down the fall, or to send a human into outer space in what is basically little more than a glorified tin can. In our eyes, those actions aren't just foolish or rash—they're *potentially catastrophic*.

And yet, luckily, a small minority of the world's population has had the curiosity, patience, and nerve to try out new ideas anyway. Thanks to these brave souls through history, we humans have gone from using primitive stone tools a few million years ago to colliding subatomic particles in the present. While the rest of the world stood on the sidelines of progress fretting about the potentially catastrophic consequences, these men and women boldly went where no one had gone before.

Sadly, many of these scientists saw their breakthroughs used not to benefit mankind, as they had intended, but to weaponize us. That theme runs through history from the time of the bow and arrow to the splitting of the atom.

Fortunately, the scientific advances have always managed to outweigh the potential catastrophies. Gunpowder, for instance, might well be the active ingredient in countless weapons, but it also helped engineers blast tunnels through mountains and clear landscapes for dams. Helicopters have become airborne gunships in modern warfare, but they also airlift injured people from the wilderness and get relief to disaster areas. The power behind the devastating atomic bomb might one day provide the world with "green" energy when we run out of oil—if we can make sure it's safe. And who can say for sure what the world-saving benefits—or the catastrophic risks—of the Large Hadron Collider will be?

Scientists have always been confident that the good they create will outweigh even the potential for catastrophe. *The Book of Potentially Catastrophic Science* lets you join them on a journey, step by step across two million years of human history. You'll get a behind-the-scenes look at just how and why those scientists could look catastrophe in the eye and not flinch. But you won't be a simple bystander—dozens of experiments will draw you into this world of probing, testing, and being amazed by the results.

Each of the 34 chapters leads off with an account of a major breakthrough or development in the world of science or technology (which is the practical application of science). You'll find them enlightening, educational, and maybe even entertaining. But by the end of each account, you'll see exactly where the potential for catastrophe lay.

What follows in each case is **THE SCIENCE BEHIND IT,** a clear explanation of the scientific principles that set the scene for the breakthrough—and opened the door for potentially catastrophic results.

And then it's time to leave the descriptions behind, roll up your sleeves, and try your hand at some wild experiments that you can do yourself. Some might require adult supervision, though, so look at the Catastrophe Meter at the top of every experiment (see chart, opposite) and proceed with care. If you do every experiment in the book, you'll have made your way through an extraordinary time line of human achievement spanning millions of years, taking you from the dawn of history, when mankind was taking its first steps on the path of science, to the measuring of tiny particles traveling at nearly the speed of light. It's an exciting trip, with lots to marvel at—if you don't spend too much time weighing the potential for catastrophe.

CATASTROPHIC METER CHART	
☢	**LOW:** No risk of catastrophe.
☢ ☢	**GUARDED:** Slight risk of mess, paper cuts, stained clothes.
☢ ☢ ☢	**ELEVATED:** Involves use of heavy or sharp objects. Adult supervision recommeded.
☢ ☢ ☢ ☢	**HIGH:** Involves use of fire, hot liquids, or hazardous substances. Adult supervision required.

The First
STONE AGE TOOLS

LET THE ARMS RACE BEGIN!

A searing sun burns a dry landscape littered with rocks and shrubs and a few dwarf trees. In the distance, beyond a great plain, are some volcanic peaks. The ash and lava from these volcanoes have enriched a soil that would otherwise be a desert wilderness. In fact, blooming plants such as sisal grow alongside different types of grasses on the vast expanse of flat land.

This is the scene that would meet you if you were transported back in time more than two million years to the Serengeti Plain in what is now Tanzania in East Africa. Plants and animals thrive in this setting, and the rich variety increases near a shallow lake, in the foreground. Just as nowadays, the animals of the African plain make their way to such expanses of open

water—and just as now, the peaceful water hole is also the scene of sudden attacks and violent kills. Powerful predators are ready to pounce on the ancestors of the wildebeests, buffalo, gazelles, and zebras that wander up to the lake to drink.

Prowling in the long grass or hidden by the lakeside trees are ancient proto-lions that are able to tackle animals much larger than themselves and kill them with one powerful clamp of their jaws. For millions of years, they have had this "menu of the day" to themselves. But now they have competition—humans.

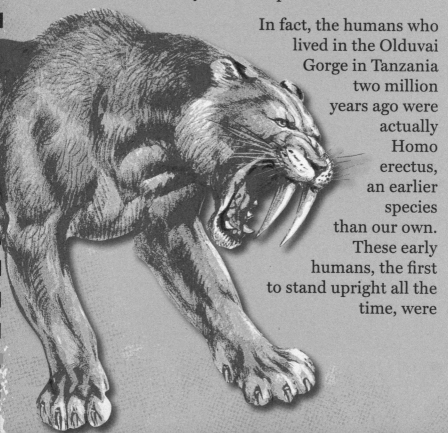

In fact, the humans who lived in the Olduvai Gorge in Tanzania two million years ago were actually Homo erectus, an earlier species than our own. These early humans, the first to stand upright all the time, were hunter-gatherers who lived primarily on the fruits and berries they managed to pick—as well as the bits and pieces of meat left behind by those dangerous predators.

Those early hominids lived solely on food from plants until they used their powerful intelligence to make a breakthrough: They began to shape stones into tools. At first they used these tools to chop up plants or dig for roots, but as time went on, they realized they could use them to hack into dead animals to get at their meat or to crack open bones to extract the nourishing marrow.

Who knows how much time passed before those first hominids realized that these very handy stone tools could also be turned into weapons? A day? A thousand years? However long it took, the same intelligence that led humans to make tools in the first place showed them how to use the stone tools as weapons. Now, in defense of early man, we can hypothesize that these weapons were purely defensive at first (ever try fending off a sabertooth cat with your bare hands? A nice sharp point would come in handy at such times). But after realizing those same stone weapons could be used to hunt and kill animals for food, it probably didn't take long for humans to turn those weapons on each other. That's when mankind's first invention took on "potentially catastrophic" proportions. The "arms race" had begun.

Hypothesis: an unproved theory that uses available evidence to explain certain facts.

THE SCIENCE BEHIND IT

THE OLDUVAI GORGE HAS BECOME ONE OF THE most fascinating sites for archaeologists looking for clues about life on Earth in the very distant past. The treasure trove that they have discovered, especially the evidence of those early humans, has given the Gorge the nickname "Cradle of Mankind." Examining this evidence further shows something else—those early humans were already using tools of scientific observation to make some important advances.

Scientists have carefully dated and examined dozens of stones found near what would have been the shores of the lake (it dried up 500,000 years ago). And it becomes clear that many of the stones dating from at least two million years ago were used as tools. The edges of these stones have been chopped away to make them sharper—or possibly chipped away so that sharp stone fragments would flake off. Using powerful microscopes to examine marks along many fossilized bones found at the Gorge, scientists have discovered that those marks match the grooves left when stone tools drag along the surface of the bone. That seems to be evidence enough for us to conclude that those early humans had used stone tools in their daily lives—to find or prepare food.

More evidence has been gathered by taking a closer look at some very remote societies existing in the world today. People in remote parts of Papua New Guinea and the Amazon rain forest make similar stone tools as the early hominids did using nothing but what they find in nature. These stone tools, known as choppers, are made by a craftsman holding one stone (the core) in his hand while striking its edges sharply with another stone. Small pieces of stone fly off, leaving the edge of the core sharper. The most basic chopper can dig out roots from hard earth. More advanced choppers, with sharpened edges, can cut through wood, animal hides, or bones.

By combining these choppers with sticks and other found objects, humans went on to make more and more sophisticated stone tools such as axes, arrowheads, and spearheads. We know that the earliest Stone Age tools were simple and made to be held in the hand, but our ancestors learned to tie the sharpened stones to pieces of wood or antler to make them more powerful. Then they would swing them down to hack at the ground or an animal bone. The longer the stick, they soon realized, the greater the force of the blow. Although they didn't know it back then, this was an example of leverage.

> **Leverage:** the mechanical advantage gained by using a lever, a rigid object (like a stick) to increase force.

Increased Force

Regular Force

Fulcrum (pivot point)

The Stone Age Chopper
EXPERIMENT 1

In this experiment you will be making your own Stone Age tool. In doing so, you will learn in half an hour what may have taken your ancestors centuries to grasp: A rock is much more effective when attached to a stick. The extra length of the stick increases the force of each swing. That's because the handle on your tool is actually a kind of lever. Your arms and shoulders, by swinging the stick, act as a fulcrum or pivot point for the lever.

MATERIALS

- **FLAT PIECE OF STONE (ABOUT THE SIZE OF A BAR OF SOAP)**
- **1 STICK (ABOUT 1 INCH WIDE AND 16 INCHES LONG); IT SHOULD BE FLEXIBLE AND STRONG**
- **SHARP WOODEN WEDGE (THE TYPE USED AS A DOORSTOP)**
- **FOUR 2-FOOT LENGTHS OF ROPE**
- **GLOVES**
- **FRIEND**

TAKE CARE!

It is a good idea to have several lengths of stick gathered beforehand in case you accidentally cut through the first stick rather than split a gap inside it. Be careful swinging the ax, because even the best Stone Age knot can come loose.

1 Hold the stone in your hand to get a feel for its shape and decide which side would be more effective as a cutting or digging instrument. A Stone Age craftsman would sharpen that side with some blows from another stone, but you don't have to (unless you want a *really* sharp tool).

2 Position the pointed edge of the wedge about halfway along the middle of the stick. Although axes and hammers have their "choppers" on top of the "stick," our ancestors had to settle for the middle of the stick so they could ensure a reasonably tight fit.

3 Put on gloves and then use the flat side of the stone as a hammer to drive the wedge into the stick.

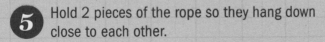

4 Keep hitting until you have split the stick so there is a gap long enough for the stone to slip inside.

5 Hold 2 pieces of the rope so they hang down close to each other.

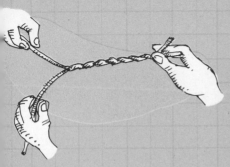

6 Have your friend crisscross the rope again and again until you've reached the bottom. This strengthened double rope is called cordage. Ancient man used to make it from plant stems, reeds, weeds, or even tough grass, and it is the earliest form of rope.

7 Repeat steps 5 and 6 to create a second length of cordage.

8 Slide or push (this may require some brute "caveperson" strength, by the way) the stone inside the slit in the stick as high as it will go and tie a piece of cordage around the branch at each end to secure it. A good double knot should work well enough to secure it.

9 You've now created a Stone Age tool Fred Flintstone would be proud of. Yabba dabba doo!

Humans
MASTER FIRE

TAMING THE MOST FEARED NATURAL FORCE

The grasslands of the South African plateau, near today's Johannesburg, provided a rich source of food for the early humans who lived there more than a million years ago. Evidence shows that groups of people carved stones and animal bones to dig for nourishing roots and insects. They would also have been able to gather berries and fruit from scrub trees growing near water holes. And the network of caves in that region offered protection against the blazing sun, heavy seasonal rains, and menacing predators that patrolled the plains and hills. One of

those predators was the Megantereon, an ancestor of the saber-tooth cat. Scientists have examined Megantereon skeletons from more than a million years ago and found evidence that the creature included humans as part of its diet.

This Megantereon skull shows exactly why early humans were virtually defenseless against these predators: Check out the size of those canines!

The humans had very few natural defenses against such killing machines. They were weaker and slower than other animals. We know they had developed primitive stone tools and some made of wood or bone, but these were virtually useless against an attack from a Megantereon. Why weren't those early human communities simply wiped out? It seems that they coupled scientific observation with courage to tame the one force that would stop even a Megantereon in its tracks—fire.

Two of the killers that hunted down their prey in ancient times are still common in southern Africa today: the leopard and the spotted hyena. Although the Megantereon became extinct some 500,000 years ago, the leopard and spotted hyena still prowl the South African plateau in search of antelope, deer, and other large mammals.

Conclusive scientific evidence shows that early humans built campfires in the mouths of caves and in other shelters as a way of protecting themselves from attack. No doubt those humans were initially as scared of fire as animals were, but being able to overcome that fear—and to tame fire in the process—was a testament to good ol' human ingenuity and pluck. No other animal in the history of the planet ever learned to "play with fire," but it was this ability to control nature's most destructive force that gave our ancestors the advantage they needed to get ahead in the struggle to survive. Not only did they learn to use fire defensively to protect themselves from predators but they used it to keep warm. They also learned to cook with it, which probably saved them from nasty diseases and ultimately prolonged their lives. With age comes wisdom, as they say (it's always older people who say that, by the way), so prolonged lives meant that old people could pass their wisdom on to younger generations.

Of course, it didn't take too long before we humans realized that fire had its potentially catastrophic side, too. After all, those who play with fire often get burned. Picture the first human to have the brilliant idea of moving the campfire inside his cave, for instance—hopefully he made it out without breathing in too much deadly smoke!

THE SCIENCE BEHIND IT

IT IS ALMOST CERTAIN THAT HUMANS HAD discovered how to use fire at different places—and in very different landscapes—at about the same time, between 1 million and 1.6 million years ago. Evidence gathered from around Swartkrans Cave in South Africa has helped us get a clearer picture of just how those early humans first came to use fire.

ya got a bone to pick?

Professor Anne Skinner of Williams College in Massachusetts uses the modern tools of chemistry to examine wood, bone, shell, and other substances that are millions of years old. She concluded that some bones found at the mouth of Swartkrans Cave were about 1.5 million years old. These bones had obviously been burned, but Dr. Skinner's tests showed that they had been burned at a particularly high temperature. That meant they had either been mixed in with a log of burning hardwood, which can quickly reach extreme temperatures in a fire, or they had been part of a fire made of dried grass and twigs that had burned long enough to reach that same heat.

Now, because that area had never had hardwood trees, the "burning log" theory was ruled out. That left only one other answer: Human beings must have noticed a brushfire caused by a lightning strike and brought some burning brush to the mouth of their cave. Then they kept feeding the fire with sticks and dried grass until they had a nice big hot blaze.

The bones that were tossed onto the fire remained long after any trace of the grass or brush had disappeared. With those bones was the proof that humans had come to tame one of nature's most fearsome elements.

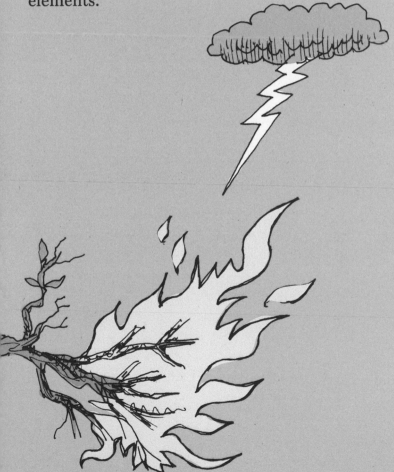

The Fahrenheit 451
EXPERIMENT 2

You can learn more about the properties of fire in the following experiment in which you'll be cooking with paper over a fire. Say what? That's right: It *is possible* to boil water in a paper cup over an open flame. The trick is knowing the "kindling point" of what you intend to burn: That is the lowest temperature at which a solid will spontaneously combust. For paper to burn, it must warm up to its "kindling point," which is 451 degrees Fahrenheit. A candle's flame would normally heat paper to that temperature, but the water inside the cup draws heat away from the paper. That keeps the paper below its kindling point while the water itself heats up to the boiling point.

MATERIALS

- PAPER CUP (MUST BE UNWAXED)
- FORK (TO POKE HOLES IN THE CUP)
- 2-FOOT LENGTH OF STRING
- TAPE
- 6–8 TEXTBOOKS
- CANDLE
- WATER
- MATCHES OR LIGHTER

MATCH ALERT!
This experiment involves the use of matches and should be conducted only with a responsible adult present.

TAKE CARE!

This experiment requires a great deal of patience, since it takes a long time to get water to boil using just a candle. Also, make extra sure that the cup you're using is unwaxed. Why? Because this experiment is all about heat passing through the paper to the water that will absorb it. If you were to use a waxed cup, the wax would absorb some of the heat that should have been absorbed by the water but in a much smaller (and therefore easier to heat up) volume ... increasing the chances of the paper itself catching fire. Also be careful that your candle doesn't get anywhere near the textbooks—or your hands!

1 Poke 2 small holes opposite each other near the top of the cup.

2 Thread the string through the cup so there is a similar amount on each side of it.

3 Make 2 piles of textbooks, each about 10 inches tall. Make sure they are both the same height, give or take a ¼ inch. Place them 16 inches apart.

4 Suspend the cup on the string between the 2 book piles, anchoring it in place on either end by sandwiching the string between the top 2 books on either side.

5 Make sure the string remains very taut. You might want to secure the ends with some tape to make sure the string stays in place.

6 Position the candle below the cup with a 2-inch gap between the candlewick and the base of the cup.

7 Fill the cup about ¾ full with water.

8 Light the candle.

9 The water will heat up and eventually boil—but the paper cup won't catch fire!

The
BOW AND ARROW

THE FIRST WEAPON OF MASS DESTRUCTION?

The Paleolithic Era, or Old Stone Age, contains about 99 percent of all human history. But by the time it drew to a close, about 10,000 years ago, humans had still not invented reading and writing. That means scientists must look at other evidence to learn how people lived in those prehistoric times. Luckily for them, our ancestors left behind loads of material for them to pore over.

Because of this, we now know that by the end of the Old Stone Age, humans were living in organized groups that hunted for food, gathered up plants, and sheltered together. Their stone tools had advanced far beyond the first choppers (see pages 1–7) into axes, knives, and, eventually, spears. These weapons could chop, slice, and stab animals faster than ever before—and (by using spears) from greater distances.

But there was one problem with these weapons: The prey knew it was being hunted. As good as a spear was, someone had to actually throw the thing, which required a fair amount of space to "throw" in. By then the woolly mammoth would have had a good chance of running away. You could practically hear the frustrated hunter's lament: "Can't someone invent something better than this? Something that could be sent zinging silently across great distances before hitting home? Oh, woe is me!"

Picture the first genius to come up with the answer. He (or she!) must have watched how the branches of some trees could be pulled back and then released to send something flying through the air at great speeds. He (or she!) must have noticed that the innards of the deer and antelope they killed in the hunt were filled with tough, stringy sinews that held the muscles to the bone. Since observation lies at the heart of true scientific progress, this truly bright inventor must have had a "eureka" moment the day he (or she!) thought of combining a wooden tree branch with a stringy sinew to create the first bow, which could then be used to send mini spears—the first arrows—flying.

This invention revolutionized the way early man killed his prey, giving him the advantage of stealth to be used not only on the hunted but also against other hunters. That's right—another invention with potentially catastrophic consequences. By the time written records did develop, the bow and arrow was established as the first killing machine—and humans were often the victims.

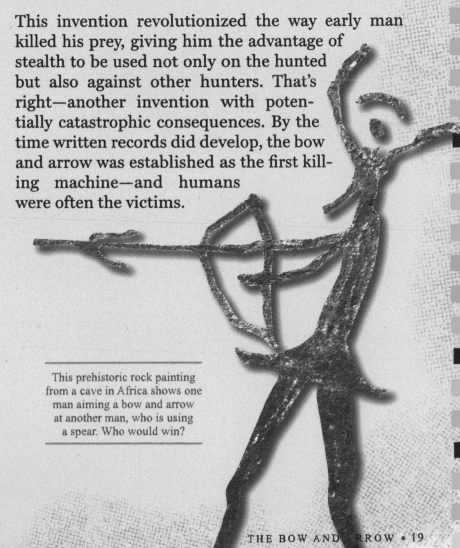

This prehistoric rock painting from a cave in Africa shows one man aiming a bow and arrow at another man, who is using a spear. Who would win?

THE SCIENCE BEHIND IT

A MODERN MILITARY EXPERT WOULD DESCRIBE a bow and arrow as a "weapons delivery system" because it involves a combination of elements. Of course, a hand throwing a stone or spear could also be described this way, but the bow and arrow takes the same principle much further. The strength of the bow, bent back as the string is pulled tighter and tighter, is much greater than that of a person's throwing arm. Even a baseball pitcher like Tim Lincecum wouldn't be able to match the power of a basic bow.

> Tim Lincecum is known for a two-seam fastball that can reach upward of 90 mph.

The strength of the bow and arrow comes from the way energy is stored, transferred, and then released. As the hunter pulls back on the bowstring, potential energy (energy that is ready to be used later) is stored in the bow. When he releases the string, this energy is quickly converted to kinetic energy (the energy of movement). This energy propels the arrow forward at great speed.

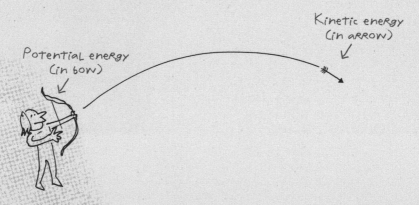

Kinetic energy (in aRROw)

Potential energy (in bow)

The bigger the bow, the more potential energy is stored and the greater the speed and distance reached by the arrow. Over the course of thousands of years, humans experimented with bows to make them stronger or faster or more accurate to suit their needs. Warriors on horseback quickly learned that small portable bows worked best for them, while ancient crossbows were so efficient they could take out small armies of men. English archers used "longbows" as tall as themselves to wipe out French armored knights in the Battle of Crécy in 1346.

In the Battle at Crécy, the English army's use of longbows helped them defeat the French, even though they were outnumbered by more than three to one.

The Mini Bow and Arrow
EXPERIMENT 3

In this experiment you will be making your own mini bow and arrows with bamboo skewers and some Silly Putty. By trying different-sized bows—and different types of arrows—you'll learn how bows and arrows evolved over time. The scientific principle behind all bow and arrows is the same: the transfer of one type of energy to another. When you pull back the string, causing the bow to bend, you build up potential energy (the type that is waiting to be used). Releasing the string turns this potential energy into kinetic energy, the energy of movement. You should be able to measure how far your different bows send their arrows and note how larger bows store up more potential energy, leading to greater kinetic energy and distance.

MATERIALS

- SCISSORS
- FOUR 12-INCH BAMBOO SKEWERS (THE KIND USED FOR MAKING SHISH KEBABS)
- SHARP KNIFE
- SILLY PUTTY
- 5 RUBBER BANDS

TAKE CARE!

Never, ever aim these or any other bows at anyone else. Also, although the bows are small, they can still send out arrows with some real force. Make sure there's nothing breakable near you—or the weapons.

1 Use the scissors to cut the sharp ends off your skewers.

2 Slice a notch in both ends of one skewer. This will be the bow.

3 Slice a notch in one end of the second skewer. This will be the arrow.

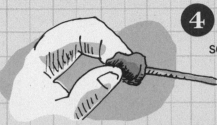

4 Place a little wad of Silly Putty at the other end of the second skewer.

5 Connect 3 rubber bands using two square knots.

6 Slide one end of the rubber-band chain into one of the slits on the "bow" and then connect the other end to the other slit.

7 The bow is now ready. Fire it by sliding the notched end of the second skewer into the middle of the rubber-band chain, then pull back and release. Measure the distance your arrow travels from a specific place. Note it down.

8 Make a second bow using a shorter bamboo skewer. Instead of 3 rubber bands, try using only 2 to make a much tauter "string" on your bow.

9 Using the same "arrow" you used for your bigger bow, shoot the arrow from the same place as before and measure the distance the arrow travels. Is it more or less?

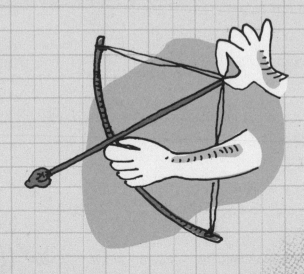

The SUMERIAN WHEEL

WHAT GOES AROUND, COMES AROUND

The Sumerian civilization thrived in Mesopotamia ("the land between the rivers" in what is now Iraq) between 3500 B.C. and 1900 B.C. This land, irrigated and enriched by the Tigris and Euphrates rivers, has always been ideal for farming. The Sumerian civilization blossomed in this setting, largely by harnessing scientific and technological advances.

One of those advances was something we take for granted whenever we ride a bike, go for a spin in a car, or take the train— the wheel. The Sumerians invented the

wheel for very practical reasons. They wanted a fast way
to produce pottery to hold
oils and grain. The potter's
wheel, which uses a spinning
plate with the clay rotating
on it, was the answer. Then
the Sumerians saw that
they could turn the wheel
upright, and if they put two
of them under a platform, they
had a cart for transporting goods.

A potter's wheel spins horizontally—
parallel to the ground—with some
moist clay placed at the center of the
spinning wheel. The potter shapes
the spinning clay with her palms and
fingers, usually working from the inside
out to widen the mouth of the pot or
to squeeze the clay to make the sides
inch higher.

Until then, farmers taking their goods to market
or to other Sumerian cities would pile goods on a
flat wooden platform that would then be dragged
along the road by donkeys or oxen. Putting wheels
under the platform and changing it into a cart
made it much easier for the animals to pull their

These details from a stone discovered in
the Royal Cemetery at Ur (c. 2500 B.C.) depict
the use of wheeled carts and chariots.

loads. They could transport more goods—and more quickly—with these wheeled carts.

Making perfectly round pots quickly and getting grain to market on a cart was all well and good, but what Sumerian rulers wanted was some way to put this new invention to use where it mattered—on the battlefield. And that was how the chariot was born, an invention with catastrophic consequences to the poor warriors who found themselves on the wrong end of a battle with ancient Sumer. Imagine the first warriors to set eyes on a battalion of ox-drawn chariots heading right at them—the thundering of thousands of hooves, the squeaking of . . . what the heck is that round thing anyway? They were probably struck down before they ever found the answer to that question.

Although the first Sumerian chariots lacked the speed of later horse-drawn versions (it would be 2,000 years before horses came to be used)—those first chariots enabled the warriors inside them to move into the ranks of their enemies, where they could pick off soldiers with their bows and arrows one by one (see previous chapter). The combination of the bow and arrow and the wheel sure must have seemed like the ancient world's version of a weapon of mass destruction.

THE SCIENCE BEHIND IT

ALTHOUGH THE SUMERIANS WERE THE FIRST TO develop the wheel, other societies made the same technological advance independently—but later. Archaeologists believe that the Sumerians invented the wheel because of their strong pottery tradition. Potters had to go all around a bowl many times, patting it down and smoothing it with their hands. But then some smart Sumerian had the notion of putting the clay on a wheel that spins around, so that the potter's hands were able to move gently against the spinning clay to shape it and smooth it without having to rotate 360 degrees all around it.

Stone slabs for potter's wheels were attached to an axle, which pointed up. Maybe that same smart Sumerian accidentally turned the wheel-and-axle on its side one time, so that the stone wheel rolled along the ground. Or perhaps some clumsy potter once knocked a piece of wood or clay under the spinning wheel, causing it to bounce up and then roll off. Who knows what the inspiration was, but whatever it was, it took a scientifically minded person to figure out that two wheels were better than one. Two wheels could be connected by a single axle and then rolled while upright. The axle could be attached to a flat platform to raise it off the ground, making the world's first cart. The Sumerians painted many images of these early carts. Farmers

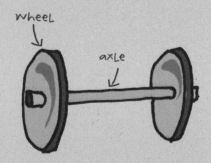

THE SIX SIMPLE MACHINES

Screw: an inclined plane wrapped around a cylinder.

Lever: a rigid bar that moves about a fixed point called a fulcrum.

Inclined Plane: a sloping surface that connects two points together.

Wheel and Axle: a wheel with a rod (the axle) running through its center.

Pulley: a machine that changes the direction of a force using a rope, chain, or cord wrapped around a wheel.

Wedge: an object with at least one slanting side ending in a sharp edge, helping to push (or cut) things apart.

would have observed that adding a second pair of wheels let the cart, now more formally a wagon, hold more and go faster.

A wheel and axle combination forms the basis of one of the six simple machines—that's what scientists call mechanisms that change the direction or magnitude (strength) of a force. For example, force that you might exert on a wheel (turning it around) can be increased at the axle. That is how people crank the handle (wheel) of an old-fashioned well to hoist a heavy bucket of water from far below. Wheels gain a type of stability called angular momentum as they spin. Momentum can be said to be a measurement of how hard it is to stop something. Angular momentum applies to objects that are spinning, like wheels. The faster a wheel is spinning, the more it wants to remain in the same plane—whether it's up and down or sideways. That is why it's easier to balance yourself on a bike when you're going fast than when you're hardly moving at all: That's angular momentum, and it's the same principle that keeps the Earth spinning, and planets, and stars, and black holes.

The Sumerian Wheel and Axle
EXPERIMENT 4

This experiment will show you a bit more about how a wheel and axle work as a simple machine by lifting a heavy object—in this case, a bucket of water. It may not seem revolutionary as a science experiment, but try to picture yourself thousands of years ago seeing a contraption like this for the first time: It would have blown you away. After you've done the experiment, try lifting the same bucket of water with one hand and see how much of the work that simple machine did for you.

MATERIALS

- TABLE- OR COUNTER-MOUNTED MANUAL PENCIL SHARPENER

- A BUCKET (THE KIND YOU USE TO MAKE SANDCASTLES) WITH A HANDLE

- STRING

TAKE CARE!
There's no real risk involved with this experiment, but it might take a little practice to get the bucket of water to lift off the ground without spilling any of it.

1 Take the outer cover off the pencil sharpener.

2 Fill the bucket ¾ full with water.

3 Cut a length of string long enough to reach from the sharpener to the floor and tie one end of it to the axle of the sharpener.

4 Tie the other end of the string to the handle of the bucket. Slowly turn the handle of the sharpener until the string becomes taut, and then continue to turn steadily as it lifts the bucket of water off the ground.

The Sumer Super Bike
EXPERIMENT 5

This experiment is a quick demo involving nothing more than the front wheel of your bike, a broom, and some string—but it's a perfect way to demonstrate the principle of angular momentum. And, you may just astound your friends while you're at it.

MATERIALS

- TWO 4-FOOT LENGTHS OF STRING
- BICYCLE WHEEL (THE FRONT WHEEL OF A SMALL BIKE WORKS BEST)
- BROOMSTICK
- 2 FRIENDS OF THE SAME HEIGHT
- SCISSORS

TAKE CARE!

Remember that as the wheel slows down, gravity will eventually overcome the angular momentum that kept it "afloat." Make sure you are able to control the wheel, so that it doesn't go rolling into something breakable. Also make sure your fingers don't get too close to the spokes of the wheel, especially once it's spinning fast.

1 Tie the ends of one piece of string together so you have a closed circle of string. Tie the other piece of string in the same way. You should have 2 loops of string.

2 Loop both pieces of string onto the broomstick.

3 Have both of your friends lift the broomstick onto their shoulders. Your friends should be facing each other.

4 Pick the wheel up and place it in between the 2 loops of string. Attach the strings to each side of the axle so that the wheel is suspended from the broomstick.

5 Start spinning the wheel as fast as you can. Remember, the wheel is being supported on its left and right sides by the string.

6 Ask your friends what will happen if you were to cut one of the strings holding the wheel. Common sense will lead them to answer that the wheel will fall.

7 While the wheel is spinning, cut one of the strings supporting it.

8 The wheel will not fall but will continue to spin in place. It will look as if it is hanging in the air, defying gravity.

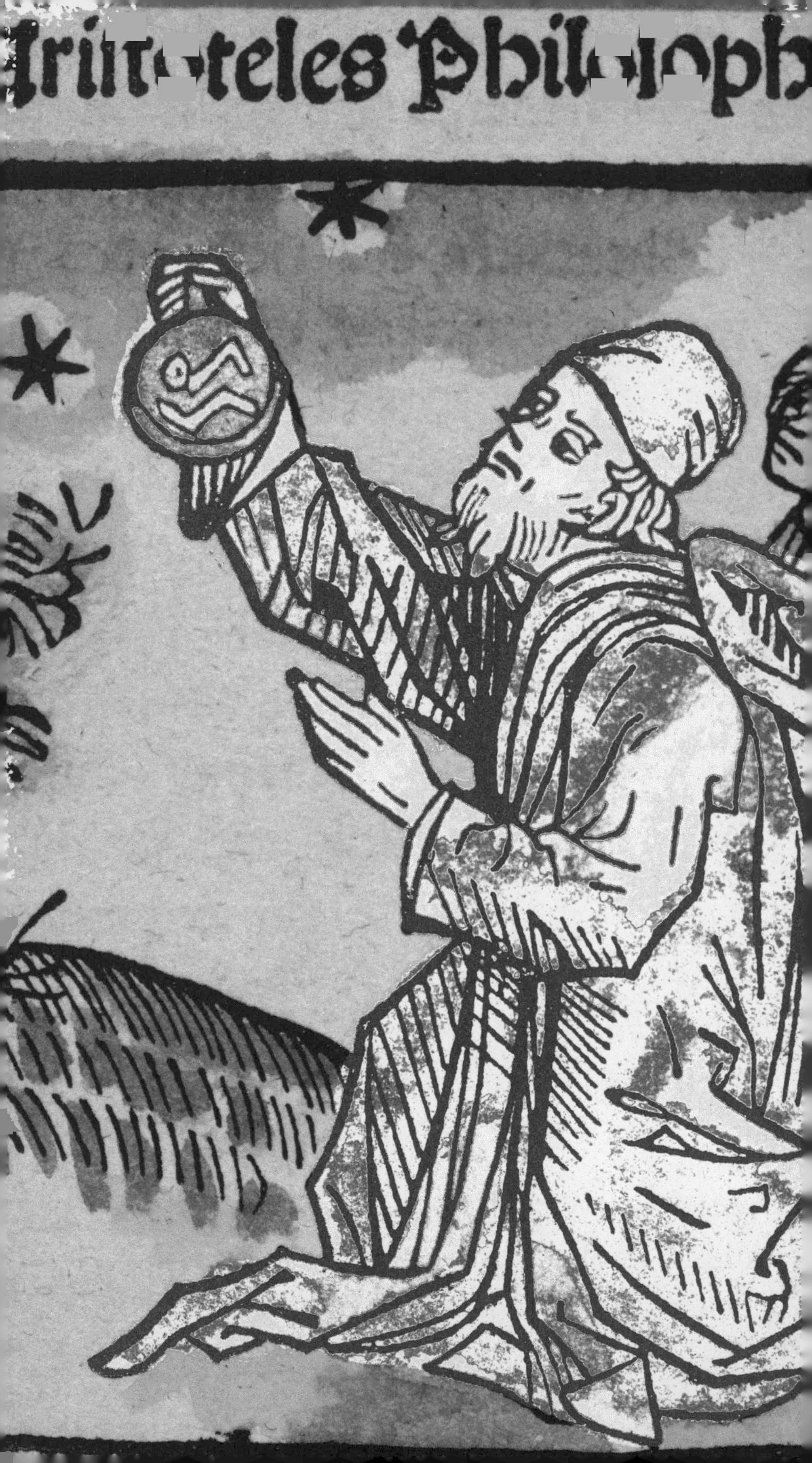

Aristotle Proclaims:
EARTH IS NOT FLAT!

THERE BE DRAGONS???

Even young children nowadays understand that the Earth is shaped more or less like a ball. Of course, you can correct that statement and say that the Earth is not really round; its shape is more like a ball that has been squeezed slightly at the north and south poles. But the main thing is that the surface of the planet is round and that if you kept traveling in the same direction, eventually you would return to the place where you started.

A few thousand years ago, though, people didn't know this simple basic fact. They believed that the surface of the Earth was flat. It's not hard to understand why they would believe this. After all, there are very few obvious clues to tell us that the Earth isn't flat. This wrong idea continued to be widely believed well into the era of ancient civilizations. The Babylonians, Egyptians, and other societies certainly believed it, as did the first Greek scholars to consider the subject about 2,800 years ago.

Imagine living in a world where people lived in fear of what would happen if you sailed over the horizon. Surely the disappearance of a ship in the distance was proof that the Earth had an edge? As a result, sailing vessels hugged the coastline, trying not to lose sight of land.

Gradually, though, some great thinkers came to conclude that the Earth was actually round and not flat. In about 330 B.C., the great scientist Aristotle noted that travelers voyaging well to the south from his native Greece saw familiar southern constellations (patterns of stars) rise higher in the sky. That would happen only if the Earth was shaped like a sphere, so he began some scientific observations of the Moon during lunar eclipses. He noted that the shadow of the Earth on the Moon was always round, but that if the Earth were flat, the shadow would be shaped like an ellipse. This confirmed to him that the Earth had to be shaped like a sphere.

About a hundred years later, another Greek, Eratosthenes (276 B.C.–194 B.C.), went one better than Aristotle: He was able to calculate the circumference of the Earth by noting the differing angles of shadows cast during the summer solstice. Then about

200 years later, yet another Greek, Strabo, recorded that sailors noticed the tops of tall mountains and buildings first as they arrived somewhere—evidence that the horizon was curved.

Now, how were any of these scientific observations potentially catastrophic in the least? It depends on how far you want to push the concept. While the ancient world was more open to these radical ideas about the Earth than it would be in Galileo's day (see pages 72–73), it took a lot of guts—and a huge leap of faith—for early sailors to actually defy the conventional wisdom at the time and sail off into the horizon. For hundreds of years, people continued to live in fear of what lay at the edges of the Earth. European maps from the Middle Ages wrote "There Be Dragons" to denote what they believed lay waiting for sailors who strayed too far from the coasts. "There Be Dragons" was simply their way of saying: "Beware: Potential Catastrophe Awaits Those Who Believe the Earth Is Round."

On medieval maps, dragons were used to indicate unknown regions or unexplored territories.

THE SCIENCE BEHIND IT

IT'S EASY TO UNDERSTAND WHY THE ANCIENT WORLD believed the Earth was either flat—or at best round but two-dimensional like a DVD—so that sailors would fall off the edge of the Earth if they sailed too far away from the center. It makes sense when you look out at the horizon and see a flat line going left to right where the sky meets the Earth. It's hard to envision how that horizon could actually be curved when you can't see it with your naked eye. The ability to work out why sailors would remain safe no matter how far away they sailed represented a breakthrough in scientific thinking. The "scientific method" as we know it involves observing, recording the results, deciding on just what those results mean, and then sharing the conclusions with others. Coming up with a line like "Chill out—you won't fall off" also involved using a lot of imagination.

> **Empirical evidence:** evidence that is based on direct observation or personal experience rather than simply theories and predictions.

When we picture a white-coated scientist pouring all sorts of strange liquids into test tubes, it's easy to understand the scientific method at work. The things being tested are right in front of the scientist, so he doesn't have to use his imagination to see what happens. It's a bit harder to understand the scientific method at work when it's all theoretical and we don't have the luxury of picking up a "flat planet" at the market to compare it to a "round planet" at home.

Instead, those early Greek thinkers looked for clues and evidence around them. They noticed that the Earth's shadow, as it crept across the Moon during an eclipse, was curved, and that the position of the stars gave clues about the planet's shape.

The Aristotle Skyscraper
EXPERIMENT 6

You can follow in the footsteps of the great Greek thinkers by putting their theories to the test (using your own empirical evidence) in this experiment, which is really a simple update of the observations that Strabo recorded about 2,000 years ago. The main difference is that he was basing his conclusions on people traveling in ancient Greek sailing vessels, and you'll be basing your conclusions on observations you're making from the backseat of your car. That's why you need to wait to do this experiment till you're going on a drive to a city that has skyscrapers—or anywhere with buildings that are more than 15 stories tall. The best time to gather your empirical evidence is when you're leaving the city.

MATERIALS

- CAR WITH OTHER PASSENGERS INSIDE IT
- CITY WITH SKYSCRAPERS OR OTHER TALL BUILDINGS
- ROAD (PREFERABLY STRAIGHT) LEADING OUT OF THE CITY

TAKE CARE!

This simple experiment is lots of fun—and informative—whenever you do it. But for the best effect, try to choose a day with clear weather so that the image of the building remains sharper and easier to describe.

1 Choose one of the tallest buildings in the city and get others in the car to choose their own. Ask the driver to note the mileage on the odometer and to tell you when you've traveled 2 miles. Observe how much of the building you can see as you begin to drive away from the city.

2 Note how much of the building remains visible at the 2-mile "observation point." Have the driver alert you every 2 miles, and note which part of the building is "lost" at each stage of the trip. What you should be realizing is that the skyscrapers will appear to be "sinking" into the ground. Of course what's really happening is that the curvature of the Earth is creating the illusion that the buildings are slowly disappearing—you're looking straight out from your car, but there's more and more curve as you travel, and it's the bottom of the building that "sinks" behind the curve first. (You can get an exaggerated model of the same thing by putting a building block on a beach ball and looking back at it from the ball's surface.)

The Aristotle North Star
EXPERIMENT 7

If you lie outside at sunset on a clear night and kept looking up, you'd notice something a bit odd. The stars seem to be moving around in circles—that is, except for one. That exception is Polaris, also known as the North Star. Imagine a line drawn from the South Pole through the Earth, and then out through the North Pole. This line would point straight at Polaris. Now imagine the Earth spinning around this imaginary line: Everything else (the other stars and planets) would appear to be going around, too. Only Polaris (the point around which everything else spins) would seem to be still.

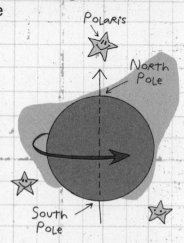

Sailors have used the position of Polaris as a way of steering ships at night because it gives them an idea of where true north is. It is a fixed point in the sky. See if you can find Polaris in your own sky.

If you can figure out how high in the sky Polaris is and then compare it with the latitude of where you are, you'll have a sense of how sailors use Polaris to figure out where they are, and help them get to where they want to go.

MATERIALS

- MAP WITH LONGITUDE AND LATITUDE MARKINGS (OR GPS OF YOUR LOCATION)

TAKE CARE!

You might need to be patient to do this experiment, especially if you live in or near a city (where lights often make it hard to see stars). Wait for a clear night when there's no moonlight (which can also dim the stars).

1 Wait at least half an hour after sunset and head for a dark spot where there's a reasonably good view of the sky.

2 First you need to find Polaris, the North Star. Look generally north and find the Big Dipper.

3 Picture an imaginary line through the two "pointer stars" of the Big Dipper; these are the two stars farthest from the Dipper's handle.

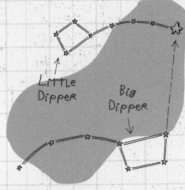

4 Follow that line (away from the "base" of the Dipper) until you see a star at the end of the handle of the Little Dipper. That is Polaris.

5 Clench both your fists and hold them straight out, with your thumbs at the top. Each clenched fist covers about 10 degrees of the sky.

6 Position one of your fists so that the horizon is beyond its bottom edge. (You might have to guess where the horizon is behind buildings, hills, or trees.)

7 Put your other fist on top of that fist and count fists as you move up, until you meet Polaris. Multiply that number by ten to get its height in degrees.

8 Now check your result against the latitude for your location. The numbers should be pretty close.

Zhang Heng's
SEISMOMETER

THE QUICK TAKE ON QUAKES?

F or as long as written accounts have existed, the Chinese have recorded terrifying and deadly earthquakes in their country. So it is not surprising that Chinese scientists have sought some way of getting warning about when earthquakes are likely to occur—and where.

One such scientist lived about 1,900 years ago. Zhang Heng was a brilliant scholar who was an accomplished writer and artist, geographer, mathematician, inventor, and engineer. He lived during a time when China was a world leader in science and technology. At the same time, however, China was always concerned about political threats from within and military attacks from beyond its borders. The emperor of China was a powerful man, of course—but he knew that his power depended on the people's confidence that he could provide protection and defense.

Zhang Heng worked for years in the imperial court in the heart of the empire. The emperor had given him the task of figuring out how to predict where earthquakes would strike next, which would enable the emperor to send relief to those areas as soon as possible. In A.D. 132, Zhang Heng presented the court with a large, ornate bronze urn. It had an elaborate title: "Instrument for measuring the seasonal winds and the movements of the Earth." It was the "movements of the Earth" bit that caught people's attention—Zhang Heng had produced a device to indicate where tremors or earthquakes were occurring, even if people at the imperial court felt no vibrations. He explained that an earthquake would cause a metal ball to drop into the top of the urn and work its way down before popping out into the mouth of one of eight carved metal toads at the base. The toads were positioned at eight compass points. If he got it right, then Zhang Heng would be

A country—or empire—as vast as China must always be on the alert to protect against foreign invasion or disaster within its own borders. The Great Wall of China, begun more than 2,000 years ago and stretching more than 5,500 miles, was a massive defense project to guard against invasion. Zhang Heng's seismometer was intended to help cope with natural disasters in far-flung parts of China itself.

able to help the emperor send emergency relief to the affected area. If he got it wrong, then political rivals (many were jealous of him) would see that he was punished—possibly with death.

The device passed the test when it correctly identified the location of the powerful Jincheng-Longxi earthquake on February 28, A.D. 138. Unfortunately, Zhang Heng died the following year, and with him went the secret of *why* and *how* his seismograph actually worked. Although modern scientists have built supersensitive seismometers to measure the strength and location of tremors and earthquakes, they still haven't been able to come up with an instrument that *predicts* when earthquakes will strike. So Chinese engineers have built models of Zhang Heng's 2,000-year-old seismometer. Maybe by studying just how it works, they will be able to figure out a way of predicting earthquakes—and averting their catastrophic consequences.

This replica of Zhang Heng's seismometer hasn't been able to explain how the original actually worked. To this day, that remains a mystery.

THE SCIENCE BEHIND IT

WE HAVE THE RECORDS THAT ZHANG HENG'S seismometer really did point toward the area of earthquake activity in A.D. 138, but everything we know about earthquakes suggests that he was right with his outcome but wrong about the science that led to it! He believed that winds caused earthquakes.

We now know that earthquakes, like volcanic eruptions, are dramatic evidence of the movement of the Earth's crust, otherwise known as plate tectonics. The Earth has four layers: the crust, the mantle, the outer core, and the inner core. The land we walk on and the seabed beneath the ocean form the thin outer layer of the Earth's crust, which is called the lithosphere. This thin layer is only about 5 to 30 miles deep, but it's where earthquakes originate. That's because the Earth's crust is not seamless, like the outside of a hard-boiled egg. It's actually much more like the outside of a hard-boiled egg that has been dropped—a lot.

Seismologists (scientists who specialize in the study of earthquakes) use highly sensitive machines called seismometers to detect and measure movements and vibrations inside the Earth. The words **seismologist** and **seismometer** come from the Greek word *seismos*, meaning "earthquake."

The shell of such an egg is still in place, but it is made up of many large and small bits that fit together like a jigsaw puzzle. Those "pieces" of the Earth's crust are called plates. The borders between these plates are called faults. Sometimes plates rest calmly against each other. At other times, though, they grind along the faults or push against each other. The word *tectonics* refers to this movement. A slight grind or push creates a vibration called a tremor. Some of these are not felt on the surface and can be picked up only by sensitive seismometers.

The Layers of Earth

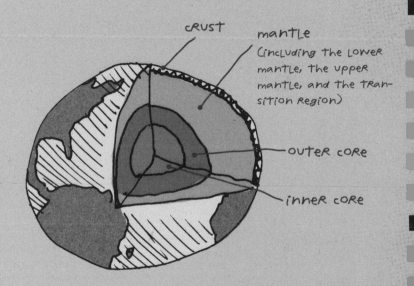

CRUST

mantLe
(incLuding the LoweR mantLe, the uppeR mantLe, and the tRansition Region)

OUTeR CORe

inneR CORe

Geology: The scientific study of the Earth; its history, origin, structure, and composition, including its rocks, soil, mountains, land formations, and fossils.

The Jell-O Earthquake
EXPERIMENT 8

In this experiment, you can make a model of plate tectonics using Jell-O! Gelatin is a great substance for creating and observing vibrations because it has a similar consistency to the molten rock that is found beneath the surface of the Earth. This molten earth, called magma, is where earthquake vibrations originate and travel. Watch how the vibrations can build up and then cause a mini earthquake in the Jell-O on the pan. You might see "faults" beginning to form and then slabs of gelatin on either side finally breaking free along those lines of weakness.

MATERIALS

- 8-INCH X 8-INCH BROWNIE PAN
- WAX PAPER
- 2 LARGE (6-OUNCE) OR 4 SMALL (3-OUNCE) PACKS OF JELL-O
- 4-PINT MIXING BOWL
- MEASURING CUP
- BUTTER KNIFE

TAKE CARE!

Make sure that you make the Jell-O a day beforehand. Considering that the making of the Jell-O isn't really part of the experiment (just a necessary first step), get an adult to do it. Plus, the adult will feel happier being the one handling the boiling water to prepare it.

(Do steps 1, 2, and 3 a day before trying out the experiment.)

1 Line the pan with wax paper. The paper should extend over the edge by 1 or 2 inches.

2 Mix the Jell-O with 4 cups of boiling water in the mixing bowl.

3 Pour the mixture into the lined pan and refrigerate for 24 hours.

4 Remove the Jell-O from the pan by pulling up on the bits of wax paper that stick out and put it on a table or counter, paper-side up. Peel off the wax paper, helping out if necessary by sliding a butter knife between the paper and Jell-O.

5 Wet the butter knife and then cut the Jell-O into two pieces.

6 Slowly slide one of the pieces along past the other piece: The border between them is like a fault on the Earth's surface.

7 Watch as the energy builds up, eventually creating tremors and maybe even a Jell-O quake.

The Chinese Alchemist's
GUNPOWDER

THE FIRST BIG BANG THEORY

t's hard for us to imagine that the most important ingredient for so many deadly weapons—gunpowder—was invented by magicians who were looking for the secret of immortality. Yet it is likely that people who seem to belong in the pages of *Harry Potter* were hard at work in ancient China, mixing strange concoctions and waiting for some fantastic results.

These scientist-magicians were called alchemists, and the subject they studied was called alchemy. Most of us have learned of European alchemists, who devoted much of their time trying to create gold and other valuable substances from more basic metals. Chinese alchemists would no doubt have welcomed the sudden arrival of gold, perhaps with a fitting puff of smoke. But their real aim was closer to the heart of anyone who has ever daydreamed: finding a way to cheat death. The sad thing is that in their efforts to overcome death, they found a quick way of taking people's lives instantly.

The Chinese have always been patient as they wait for results. Even now, people can go to Chinese markets and buy hard-boiled eggs that have been buried for 100 years to get the right flavor. Chinese alchemists were equally patient. After all, becoming immortal is worth the wait! They would mix several substances in large pots and then let them sit for up to 50 years. At the end of this period, the alchemists would test the results.

As far as we know, no one ever found the secret to living forever. But around A.D. 850, the Chinese discovered that one of their mixtures would burn very quickly—and even explode—accompanied by some brilliant colors. This mixture was what we call gunpowder.

The first gunpowder was weaker than what we now use as gunpowder, but it still produced wonderful flashes and bursts of color. The Chinese harnessed these properties to develop an invention that has delighted children ever since—fireworks. But

Firework casings today still contain most of the same ingredients as ancient Chinese gunpowder.

This dragon fountain is modeled after an ancient Chinese cannon.

before long, scientists found that they could improve the formula to produce rockets. That was still fun: Now they could launch those colorful fireworks into the sky. But catastrophe lurked in the background. If rockets can be sent zooming into the sky, they can also be aimed at people. Cannons made their first appearance not long after the first fireworks were launched. And, unfortunately, the bombs just got bigger and bigger over time.

THE SCIENCE BEHIND IT

EVEN IF THE CHINESE ALCHEMISTS WHO DISCOV-
ered gunpowder were working in the realm of what
we call magic, some of their methods were completely scientific. One of the most important features
of what is called the "scientific method" is watching an experiment closely and then making a clear
record of those observations. Each time the alchemists set up one of their "immortality" experiments,
they listed the ingredients. Very often those experiments were duds, with nothing to show for decades
of observation but a dull mixture that hasn't changed
at all—and has no special properties.

Those same alchemists struck gold (in a way) when
one set of three basic ingredients produced gunpowder. One of those ingredients, carbon, is common
throughout the world: Charcoal is a good example
of carbon. The second ingredient, sulfur, was well
known to Chinese doctors: It occurs naturally in parts
of China, and Chinese
scientists had found
ways of extracting it
from other sources
more than 2,000 years
before. The third—
and possibly most
important—ingredi-
ent of gunpowder is
potassium nitrate,
often called salt-
peter. Like sulfur,
it is found in parts

Fireworks are an excellent example of
controlled combustion. Manufacturers
deliberately keep the fuel (gunpowder)
and oxidizers (dry chemicals that
release oxygen to trigger combustion)
from being mixed together too much
and too soon. So instead of joining
together with one almighty split-
second explosion, the particles burn
for a few seconds to display the widest
range of colors.

An Explosive Formula

charcoal   SULFUR   saltpeter   oxygen

of China, and Chinese scientists had long known that it could be used to extract valuable metals from mixtures.

Scientists often test a new material to see whether—and how—it will burn. This is called combustion, the chemical reaction that occurs when something combines with oxygen to produce heat or light. In order for anything to burn, it must combine with oxygen. When this happens, energy is released—either slowly or quickly. In the case of gunpowder, the energy is released so quickly that it forms an explosion. This is because the carbon-sulfur-saltpeter mixture is mixing with the oxygen at such a fast rate that the heat it generates literally comes out as a burst of energy—and that causes the mixture to ignite.

EXPERIMENT 9

One of the best things about fireworks—apart from the amazing booms—is the way they produce such wonderful colors. But they're gone in a split second, and you're left having to remember exactly what they looked like. Here's an experiment that lets you slow down the basic process behind exploding fireworks—combustion—and lets you appreciate the changing colors for as long as you like. How? Because unlike the combustion at play in a fireworks explosion, which produces hundreds of degrees of heat, there are some forms of oxidation (the chemical reaction involving oxygen) that actually happen in slow-motion. Rusting, for instance, is one of the slowest forms of oxidation, as rusting metal gives off only about one degree Fahrenheit.

In this experiment you'll drop steel wool into a cup of vinegar and measure the temperature before and after. The secret to this experiment, of course, is the use of vinegar to remove the protective steel from the wool, which means that the iron inside the wool becomes exposed to the oxygen in the air. Even in that short time, the wool is able to oxidize (in this case, rust). Notice the reddish color on the steel wool at the end? The same science is at work behind gunpowder.

TAKE CARE!

Make sure you don't get any vinegar in your eyes. Throw away the used steel wool after you've finished the experiment, and rinse out the jar and cup before putting them into the dishwasher. Also, make sure to use a glass thermometer, the kind you can purchase at a pet supply store or from online science stores.

MATERIALS

- **GLASS JAR (ABOUT 12 FLUID OUNCES) WITH SCREW-TOP LID**

- **1 ALCOHOL THERMOMETER**
(The kind used in science classes and for lab work; they are made of glass and look like the old mercury thermometers but contain alcohol instead of mercury.)

- **VINEGAR**

- **STEEL WOOL**

- **COFFEE CUP OR MUG**

1 Put the thermometer inside the jar and close the lid.

2 Wait 10 minutes, take the thermometer out, and record the temperature.

3 Fill the cup halfway with vinegar and soak the steel wool in it for a minute.

4 Wrap the steel wool around the bulb at the base of the thermometer and put them into the jar, closing the lid.

5 Repeat step 2 and compare the 2 temperature readings.

Regiomontanus's
LUNAR ECLIPSE

HOW COLUMBUS STAVED OFF A MASSACRE IN JAMAICA

Everyone has heard of Christopher Columbus's voyage of discovery across the Atlantic in 1492. What fewer people know is that he made three more journeys to the "New World" over the next 12 years. None of these voyages, however, was as triumphant as the first. And on the last of them, which began in 1502, Columbus had to use his wits (and the scientific knowledge of a German astronomer named Regiomontanus) to save his crew from certain death.

Columbus and his men had sailed along the coast of Central America and to many

Caribbean islands at the start of that mission. By 1503, though, his ship had been damaged in heavy storms and its hull was leaking badly because of shipworm. He had to find land or they would all be lost at sea, so he landed at Saint Ann's Bay in Jamaica. The crew was safe, but they found themselves stranded on the island because of the damage.

> **Shipworm:** not a worm at all, but a tiny clam that lives in tropical waters and uses its shell to bore through wood in search of food. Shipworms are sometimes called "termites of the sea."

At first the local Native American people, the Taino, welcomed the Europeans and gave them food and shelter. Soon, however, tensions rose as Columbus's men took advantage of that kindness and began behaving cruelly toward their hosts. Eventually, the Taino turned against Columbus and his men, threatening to kill them. Columbus had to think of a way of making them change their minds so he could buy time until a Spanish rescue party could arrive.

On February 26, 1504, he had a meeting with some of the Taino leaders, telling them that the Christian god was angry with the Taino's refusal to help Columbus. And to express his anger, at sunset three days later the god was going to take the Full Moon from the sky. Many of the Taino laughed at this announcement, but three days later they assembled to watch the Moon rise. Sure enough, it began to turn color (another Columbus prediction) and then slowly it seemed to be eaten away. Terrified, the leaders asked Columbus to plead with his god. Columbus agreed, but only on the condition that they would help him.

Columbus greets the Taino natives
on the island of Jamaica in 1503.

He went away briefly and then returned, saying that
his god forgave them. Within about 40 minutes the
moon began to grow fuller and eventually was whole
again.

The Taino gratefully continued to supply Columbus
and his men, who were rescued by a Spanish ship
four months later.

THE SCIENCE BEHIND IT

WHAT COLUMBUS PREDICTED—AND JUST IN THE nick of time—was a lunar eclipse. Like many navigators of that time, Columbus had a well-thumbed copy of an almanac written by the German astronomer Regiomontanus. That book contained details of the movements of the Sun, Moon, and planets for the period 1475 to 1506. And among the many astronomical events it covered were solar (of the Sun) and lunar (of the Moon) eclipses.

Sensing trouble and looking for some way to impress the Taino chiefs, Columbus must have rifled through the pages until he reached his date in 1504. Think of how lucky he was to have found an eclipse about to happen so soon afterward!

Eclipses are all about movement and light. A solar eclipse occurs when the Moon passes in front of the Sun. Sometimes its path leads it across only part of the Sun—such events are called partial eclipses. A total solar eclipse is much rarer and is remarkable because the Moon seems to fit exactly over the disk of the Sun. That is because the Sun is 400 times

Regiomontanus (Johannes Müller von Königsberg).
(Geb. 6. Juni 1436, gest. 6. Juli 1476.)

Portrait of Johannes Müller von Königsberg, better known as Regiomontanus, who died mysteriously at the age of 40. Some say he died of plague. Others say he was assassinated by his enemies. Did his scientific discoveries have anything to do with his death?

larger than the Moon but 400 times farther away. You can see this effect by holding your arm outstretched with your thumb pointing up. Your thumb might exactly cover a tree in the distance although you know that the tree is much, much bigger.

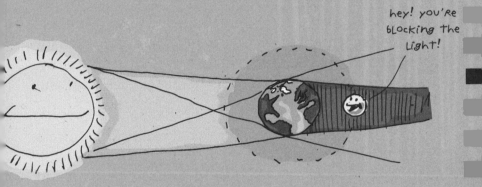

hey! you're blocking the light!

Lunar eclipses, like the one Regiomontanus predicted, happen when the Earth blocks the Sun's light from reaching the Full Moon. Such eclipses are far more common than solar eclipses, plus they can be seen from anywhere on Earth (only a tiny portion of the Earth can see a total solar eclipse). Because the apparent paths of the Sun and the Moon can be tracked and predicted from Earth, keen observers of celestial bodies like Regiomontanus have been able to note patterns and forecast when eclipses will occur, decades or even centuries into the future.

Regiomontanus's Orange Lunar Eclipse
EXPERIMENT 10

This experiment—best performed in a darkened room—is a great way to learn about the phases of the Moon and how they relate to eclipses. The phases, describing how much of the Moon is illuminated, are evidence that the Moon orbits the Earth. Each 27.3 days the Moon makes a full circuit around the Earth. When it is closest to the Sun in its orbit we see only its darkened shape (the New Moon) because the Sun's light is all on the far side. A week or so later, half of the side we see is illuminated (the First Quarter) and then a week later all of it is bathed in light (the Full Moon). Sometimes, though, the Moon's orbit takes it through the shadow caused by the Earth itself and the face of the Moon darkens until it passes out of the shadow. These events are lunar eclipses.

MATERIALS

- A NICE ROUND ORANGE
- PENCIL
- STANDING LAMP

TAKE CARE!

Be careful not to poke your hand as you stick the pencil into the orange. When you've finished the demonstration, turn some other lights on (and open the curtains if it is daytime) and switch the standing lamp off. Don't even try to put the lampshade back on for at least 10 minutes as the bulb will remain quite hot even after you turn off the lamp.

1 Stick a pencil into the orange navel so you can hold it like a candy apple.

2 Put the lamp in the center of the room.

3 Remove the lampshade so that the bulb is exposed.

4 Turn off any other lights and turn the lamp on.

5 Start off with your outstretched arm pointing toward the lamp. You should see only the shadowy side of the orange, just as we see only shadow at the New Moon.

6 Keep holding the orange outstretched and make a quarter turn counterclockwise (to the left). This is the First Quarter Moon phase.

7 Make another quarter turn counterclockwise. (Make sure your head isn't blocking the light from hitting the orange.) This is the Full Moon phase. The orange is completely illuminated by the light.

8 Continue for a full circle until you have noted all the phases, including the crescent and gibbous phases.

9 Now, to see a lunar eclipse on your orange, go back to the Half Moon lunar phase. Adjust the height of your outstretched arm so that the shadow of the Earth (your head) covers all or part of the Moon (the orange). Do you see the lunar eclipse?

Galileo's
TELESCOPE

PHYSICS MEETS THE POWER OF THE INQUISITION

E very so often, a person comes along who shakes things up and causes us to look at the world in a new way. It might be an artist such as Pablo Picasso, or someone like Rosa Parks, whose courage changed the way a whole nation thought about itself. Science has also been enriched with the work of such special people, and one of the greatest was Galileo Galilei (1564–1642). In fact, in the words of a present-day science hero, Stephen Hawking, "Galileo, perhaps more than any other single person, was responsible for the birth of modern science."

Heresy: choosing to believe opinions that differ from those of an established religion.

Why did Stephen Hawking say that about Galileo? One of the main reasons was that Galileo pioneered what is now called the scientific method (see page 38). Rather than simply come up with vague theories about how the world operated, Galileo conducted thousands of experiments. He observed the results carefully and then did the experiments again and again before arriving at conclusions. In this way, he came up with many theories about how objects moved and the forces that lay behind that movement. In 1608, Galileo learned of a new invention (the telescope) and set about improving what was still a primitive device. By 1609, he was satisfied with his superior telescope and began using it in his studies.

On January 7, 1610, Galileo was using his telescope to study the Moon. Before going to bed, he turned his gaze to the planet Jupiter and noticed three small stars lined up next to it. When he looked the next night, the stars were on the opposite side of the planet. And when he looked a third time, they were in a new arrangement—plus there was a fourth star joining them. Galileo carefully recorded their positions and soon concluded that they were moons, revolving around Jupiter just as our Moon revolves around Earth. By seeing those planetary patterns in the solar system, it wasn't long before Galileo deduced that our own Earth was also revolving around something—the Sun.

This kind of thinking, however, was considered heresy by the Catholic Church at the time, which taught that nearly every aspect of life was part of "God's Plan" as revealed in the Bible and in Church teaching. The church was a very powerful force in Europe—and especially in Galileo's native Italy—and Galileo's assertions that the Earth was not the center of the universe threatened its very foundations. This idea, which was known as Copernicism, directly contradicted the Bible's assertion that the Sun revolved around the Earth. If this view was proven to be wrong by Galileo's discoveries, what else would be proven wrong? Galileo had to be stopped.

First came a warning (in 1616) not to write about Copernicism, although Galileo was free to discuss it. Over the next 16 years, however, he developed his ideas further and, despite the possibly catastrophic consequences that awaited him (see box, opposite, for details on what happened to Giordano Bruno, another scientist who dared to oppose the church), published his scientific discoveries in 1632. He was arrested the following year at the age of 68. Threatened with torture, Galileo was forced to renounce his views in public before being sentenced to prison. That punishment was eventually changed to "house arrest," but Galileo was never to be a free man again. He spent his last years in his house in Florence, blinded by an eye infection, and died in 1642.

Legend has it that Galileo muttered "Eppur si muove" ("and yet it moves") under his breath immediately after confessing that the Earth does not move around the Sun in 1633.

THE SCIENCE BEHIND IT

AT THE HEART OF GALILEO'S WORK WAS A BRIL-liant combination of scientific observation and mathematics. In this way, he can be said to be the Father of Modern Physics. He observed the way objects moved—being thrown or dropped, for example—and found patterns that worked out mathematically. He noted how objects accelerate (gain speed) at the same rate regardless of their mass, and he observed how gravity affected the path of moving objects. He worked patiently to test, and retest, observations before drawing conclusions that advanced our knowledge of the world. He also had the skill to present his findings clearly to the wider world—even if that skill landed him in so much trouble with the Church. And he was a skilled craftsman who took what was then an unreliable invention (a spyglass) and turned it into a precision instrument (a telescope) that could reveal wonders.

Working with different lenses, Galileo learned that magnification was proportional to the ratio of the power of the two lenses in the telescope, the one in front and the one in the back. To achieve the highest magnification possible, he needed a weak convex lens in the back and a strong concave lens in the eyepiece. The only problem was that opticians at the time didn't make the kinds of lenses he needed, so in short order Galileo learned how to grind his own lenses.

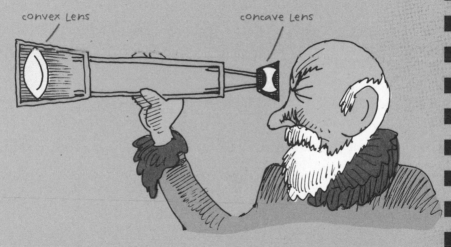

convex Lens

concave Lens

Training his telescope on Jupiter, Galileo spent four weeks analyzing what he saw through his own specially made lenses. Each night he made drawings of what he sighted, in particular what appeared to be four stars moving around the planet. He concluded that these were four moons. Even today, those four brightest moons of Jupiter are called "Galilean Moons" in his honor.

Galileo's Homemade Telescope
EXPERIMENT 11

Galileo displayed a brilliant understanding of optics (the science of how light behaves, especially as it travels through a lens) to construct his telescope in 1609. You can pick up some of the same knowledge as you follow in his footsteps in this experiment, which lets you build your own telescope. And like Galileo, you can use this new tool to observe how objects in the heavens move around one another. The orbital paths of moons—whether they are our own or those by other planets— are excellent examples of the same angular momentum that governs a spinning bicycle wheel (see page 29).

MATERIALS

- 2 PAPER-TOWEL CARDBOARD TUBES
- PENCIL
- SCISSORS
- DUCT TAPE
- POCKET MAGNIFIER (WITH CIRCULAR, NOT RECTANGULAR, LENS)
- MAGNIFYING GLASS (THE SAME WIDTH AS THE CARDBOARD TUBES)
- KNIFE

TAKE CARE!

It's important that the two lenses are parallel and secure. Be pa and prepared to adjust the duct taping in order to achieve this. Never look at the Sun through this telescope. The magnification (the amount it increases the appearance of things) of the telesco depends on the difference in size between the large and the smal lens. If your telescope seems "underpowered" to view Jupiter's moons, try looking at the edge of our own Moon along the line of the shadow. You'll still see loads of craters and valleys.

1 Use your pencil and a ruler to draw a straight line lengthwise down one of the cardboard tubes. Then use your scissors to cut along the line.

2 Overlap one edge of the cut cardboard tube about an ⅛ inch over the other edge so that it forms a slightly narrower tube. Secure it lengthwise with duct tape. This tube should now be able to slide into the other tube and feel snug. Take it out and put both cardboard tubes next to each other on a table.

3 Detach the magnifying lens from the handle and the pocket lens from its handle.

4 Use the knife to make a slit about an inch from one end of the wider cardboard tube. It should be parallel to the edge and wide enough to hold the magnifying lens. (Don't cut all the way through.)

5 Make a similar slit an inch from the end of the narrower tube, big enough for the pocket lens.

6 Slide each lens into its slot and secure the small bit that juts out to the outer surface of the tube with duct tape.

7 Slide the smaller tube into the larger so the lenses are at each end.

8 Hold this telescope up to your eye and look through the smaller lens at a distant object. Slide the tube back and forth until the object becomes clear.

Galileo's Jupiter Moons
EXPERIMENT 12

In this experiment you'll be using your homemade telescope to see those four "Galilean Moons." Scientists using much more powerful telescopes continue to find more and more of Jupiter's moons, which they prefer to call satellites. Well, if these moons are really satellites, then what do we call satellites like the ones that help transmit television signals? Those are artificial satellites.

MATERIALS

- YOUR NEWLY MADE TELESCOPE FROM THE PREVIOUS EXPERIMENT OR BINOCULARS
- SMALL PICNIC TABLE (OPTIONAL)
- NOTEBOOK AND PENCIL
- FLASHLIGHT

TAKE CARE!

Unlike Galileo, you're unlikely to be sent to jail for this bit of astronomical research. Don't ignore step 4: It can make all the difference between a blast of exciting discovery and real frustration.

1 Make sure that Jupiter is visible in your area (at some times in the year it is too low to be seen). Download a free chart from http://skymaps.com to learn if—and where in the sky—it can be seen.

2 Use the chart to help you find Jupiter with your naked eye. It is one of the brightest objects in the sky, so if it is visible, it should be easy to identify.

3 Now find it with your telescope or binoculars.

4 If you are using binoculars or a telescope without a tripod, try leaning an elbow on the table to reduce the shakiness in what you see.

5 Note the position of any small "stars" on either side of Jupiter.

6 Record those positions in your notebook (using the flashlight if you're writing outside).

7 Continue for a week or more. Can you see a pattern developing?

8 Try to predict what their positions will be in another week, or even a month. Were you right?

Isaac Newton's
FALLING APPLE

ON THE UP-AND-UP

One afternoon in 1665, while sitting in his family's orchard in the village of Woolsthorpe, England, Isaac Newton (1642–1727) noticed an apple falling from one of the trees. The motion of the apple as it hit the ground (some accounts say it hit his head), got Isaac thinking: What caused the apple to be drawn to the ground? Was there some mysterious force that drew everything toward everything else? Maybe this force could even explain why planets were drawn to the Sun. Newton began investigating this "force" and soon his calculations became so complicated that he had to invent a new type of mathematics (differential calculus) to figure it all out.

It took twelve years of research, but finally, in 1687, Newton published *Mathematical Principles of Natural Philosophy*, which offered the scientific explanation behind that mysterious force that held everything together: the Law of Universal Gravitation—otherwise known as "gravity." The book also established three important laws of motion (see page 83) to explain not just how gravity works but the effect of *any* force on an object on how it moves. These laws helped later scientists work out the location of distant galaxies, build submarines, send spacecraft to the Moon, and describe the motion of particles too small to see even with the most powerful microscopes.

All of this is wonderful, but where's the catastrophic angle? That's pretty obvious, if you think of it. It was Newton's Laws of Motion that paved the way for everything we now refer to as modern physics. Have you heard of the saying "Who let the genie out of the bottle?" It refers to the mythic "genie" in old Arabian stories, a magic spirit that lived inside a bottle who would do whatever the person who let it out of

No one can be quite sure how much of the "falling apple" story is true. Perhaps it was a simple way for Newton to explain some complicated science to ordinary people. Maybe it was just a tall tale, like the story of George Washington and the cherry tree. On the other hand, the writer William Stukeley recalled a conversation with Newton, who referred to "the fall of an apple" as a source of inspiration.

Isaac Newton once famously remarked: "If I have seen a little further, it is by standing on the shoulders of giants." This was his way of acknowledging the great contributions of the scientists who came before him.

the bottle commanded. The problem with the genie was that it was very hard to get him back inside the bottle, and he was very hard to control—meaning his magic often led to unexpected consequences. Science has always been a little like that crazy genie in a bottle. You could say that Aristotle and Galileo started uncorking the bottle years before, but it was Newton who let the genie out all the way.

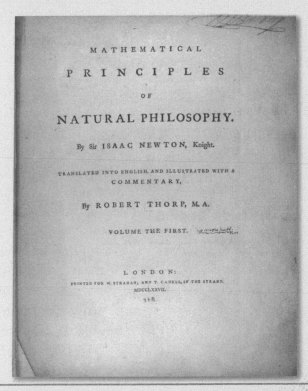

MATHEMATICAL

PRINCIPLES

OF

NATURAL PHILOSOPHY.

By Sir ISAAC NEWTON, Knight.

TRANSLATED INTO ENGLISH, AND ILLUSTRATED WITH A
COMMENTARY,

By ROBERT THORP, M.A.

VOLUME THE FIRST.

LONDON:
PRINTED FOR W. STRAHAN, AND T. CADELL, IN THE STRAND.
MDCCLXXVII.

Isaac Newton first published The Law of Universal Gravitation in this book, *Mathematical Principles of Natural Philosophy*, in 1687.

THE SCIENCE BEHIND IT

KNOW ANY GOOD POEMS ABOUT SCIENTISTS? HOW about this one:

> Nature and Nature's laws lay hid at night.
> God said, "Let Newton be!" and all was light.

These lines were part of a longer poem that Alexander Pope (1688–1744) composed in memory of Isaac Newton, just three years after the scientist's death. They tell us a lot about how quickly the general public realized the scale of Newton's achievement. Imagine a present-day poet writing about the work of Stephen Hawking or Albert Einstein.

And just what was Newton's contribution? You'd need a series of books to do his work justice, but at its core were the Law of Universal Gravitation and the three Laws of Motion. Newton stated that everything in the universe exerts a gravitational force on everything else, and that this gravitational force depended on the distance between the objects and their mass. What we call the force of gravity decreases if the distance between the objects becomes greater, but increases in proportion to their masses.

Newton's laws of motion took the work of Galileo (see page 69), whom Newton greatly admired, a stage further. Galileo had observed planets and moons and concluded that they moved. Newton showed—in clear language that even poets understood—why and how they moved.

The international unit of measure for force is the Newton, abbreviated to N.

NEWTON'S THREE LAWS OF MOTION

The **First Law of Motion** states that an object in motion will remain at the same speed and direction unless an outside force acts on it. In the same way, an object at rest (not moving) will stay at rest.

The **Second Law of Motion** explains why it takes more effort (force) to move a heavy object than a light one. It gives a formula to explain how much force is needed to change its speed or direction (known in science as acceleration):

force = mass × acceleration

The **Third Law of Motion** says that for every action there is an equal and opposite reaction. So, when a cannonball is fired (an action), the cannon itself is pushed back (a reaction). In other words, forces are found in pairs. When you sit on a chair, you are exerting a downward force; if the chair doesn't exert a matching upward force, it will collapse.

It takes more force to move a heavy object than a light one.

Newton's Science Friction
EXPERIMENT 13

This experiment is a demonstration of one of the outside forces that acts on moving objects, causing them to slow down and stop: friction. We see it at work whenever we compare, for example, a hockey puck sliding across a skating rink with the same puck sliding across a carpeted floor. But this experiment shows how friction is at work between the pages of a book, and how that force can build up astoundingly. Each overlap is a source of friction, but multiplying that force by 50, 60, or however many overlaps you managed to produce, will increase the force a great deal.

MATERIALS

- **2 PAPERBACK BOOKS OF ABOUT THE SAME SIZE AND NUMBER OF PAGES**

TAKE CARE!

No real problems here—just don't use someone's priceless first edition (even if it *is* a paperback).

1 You're aiming to "lock" the books together by having their pages overlap one another.

2 Put the books on a table, facing each other so that they just touch.

3 Lift each book up by the open-pages side so that the spines stay on the table but edge closer to each other by about 1½ inches.

4 Rifle through the pages with your thumbs (from the back of the book to the front).

5 If you've managed to do this right, the pages of the books will overlap each other by the same 1½ inches.

6 Try to pull the books apart. It seems as though they're locked together.

Newton's Third Law of Motion
EXPERIMENT 14

This is a great way to see equal and opposite forces in action (and reaction). When you let go of the holes in the carton, the water goes shooting out. That is the first force. It also pushes back on the carton with equal force, just as the fuel burning out of the back propels a rocket forward. But because you are holding the carton in place from above, the linear (straight-line) force becomes converted into a rotational (spinning) force.

MATERIALS

- EMPTY HALF-GALLON BEVERAGE CARTON
- PENCIL
- SCISSORS
- STRING
- FRIEND TO HELP AND OBSERVE
- WATER

TAKE CARE!
Make sure you do this outside, because the water will get everywhere.

1 Use a pencil to jab a hole in the bottom-left corner of each side of the carton.

2 Make a similar hole in the center of the top flap. (This might be a little too tough for the pencil, so you can use the scissors.)

3 Cut a 2-foot length of string and tie one end through the hole in the flap.

4 Hold each of the four bottom holes while your friend fills the carton with water and holds the free end of the string.

5 Get your friend to hold the string up and away from herself, and let go of the four holes.

6 Water should rush out of the holes and the carton should spin around until the water runs out.

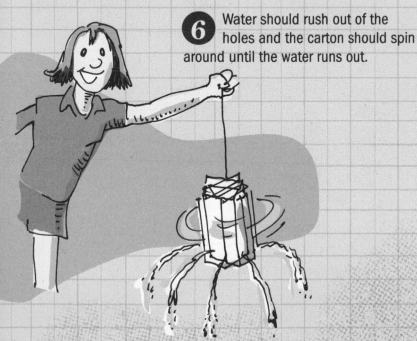

Ben Franklin's
ELECTRIC KITE
. . . AND SOMEHOW HE DOESN'T GET FRAZZLED

What is it about wild weather that brings out the daredevil in some of the wisest people? Dozens of ordinary, nine-to-five types across America spend every spring poised to abandon their work cubicles at the drop of a hat. Then they jump into their cars to become "storm chasers," tracking severe thunderstorms that they hope will develop into tornadoes.

More than 250 years ago, one of America's wisest statesmen risked electrocution in a similarly rash exercise—his aim was to unlock the secret of lightning. Talk about potentially catastrophic! Do you know what a 300,000-volt bolt of lightning can do to a person? Benjamin Franklin did not have an established track record in death-defying stunts. He was more famous for his wise sayings (in *Poor Richard's Almanack*), the invention of an efficient stove and bifocal eyeglasses, and his diplomatic efforts in the cause of American independence. But he had a lively curiosity about everything around him, and he used scientific methods to learn more and to test out ideas.

Lightning is the discharge of electricity in the atmosphere on a BIG, BIG scale. A bolt travels at 60,000 miles per second from cloud to ground and can contain up to a billion volts of electricity. Its temperature of 54,000 degrees Fahrenheit is hotter than the surface of the Sun.

By the 1750s, Franklin, like other scientists, had become convinced that lightning was really the same as static electricity, but millions of times more powerful than the shocks that people get from woolen sweaters. He also knew that lightning strikes—or seeks out—high objects. The third thing that Franklin must have known (because he could not have survived his famous experiment in the face of a full-on electrical storm) was that a static electricity charge must build up as the storm brews (the clouds become more negatively charged and everything below becomes more positively charged) and that the charge is waiting to flow from the negative to the positive because opposites attract.

With these things in mind, Franklin and his son, William, noticed dark clouds developing over Philadelphia one June afternoon in 1752. They launched a special kite that had a metal key at the end of its string. Extending from the suspended key were a ribbon (which Franklin held) and a wire leading down to a Leyden jar (which stores electrical charge).

Benjamin and William waited patiently as several clouds passed nearby: Nothing happened to the kite or the key. Then Benjamin noticed that the string leading down from the

This engraving from *The Boy's Playbook of Science* shows Ben Franklin drawing a spark off the kite string using the key.

kite had become wet . . . and possibly charged (an electrical charge would travel along a wet string far more easily). He held out his free hand to the key, but even before he touched it, there was a bright flash between the key and his hand. Franklin jumped back but wasn't hurt. He concluded that the rain-soaked string had become an electrical conductor and that some of the charge that was on its way to the Leyden jar had been diverted to his hand. A charge of that strength could only have come down from the kite, because it was so close to the highly charged storm clouds.

The **Leyden jar** takes its name from the Dutch town of Leiden, where in 1745 Pieter van Musschenbroek invented the first device to capture and store an electrical charge.

THE SCIENCE BEHIND IT

BEN WAS A WISE AND CRAFTY FELLOW, AND MANY people doubt that he ever even conducted his most famous experiment. (Mind you, these people might also doubt whether George Washington ever cut down a cherry tree.) The doubters believe that Ben Franklin *knew* that negative charges that had built up in the clouds would travel down the wet string and wire into the Leyden jar but that he would never have been silly enough to risk getting a massive electric shock himself. So, they say, he pretended to have conducted the experiment with his son because people would believe the underlying science if they thought that the kite experiment really had taken place.

Maybe you can become a scientific historian and work out whether Benjamin and William really did risk their lives on that June afternoon. But remember: Everything in the account of the day really could have happened, because Ben Franklin had understood how static electricity can build up—and how it can be discharged in the most dramatic form (lightning).

The term "static electricity" describes the sudden flow of negatively charged particles that have built up on one object across to the positively charged particles on another. As you walk across a room, for example, electrons from the carpet are rubbed off and absorbed by your body (giving you a slightly negative charge). Some of these extra electrons, on your fingers, can flow across to the positively charged particles on the surface of a metal doorknob—then you might see a spark and feel a little shock as they meet.

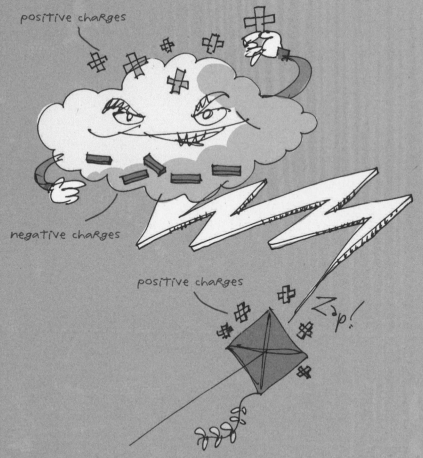

positive charges

negative charges

positive charges

Zap!

When the negatively (-) charged particles in the lower cloud jump across to meet the positively (+) charged particles on the kite below them, the result is a lightning bolt.

Lightning is an example of the same process, although on a much, much bigger scale. Ice crystals in storm clouds bounce around violently and exchange charged particles. The positively charged particles wind up on the tops of the clouds, while the bottoms of the clouds become negatively charged (like your fingers when you touch a doorknob). The buildup of negative charge is waiting to find the nearest positively charged particles, and it usually finds them on the tallest objects, such as treetops, church steeples . . . or Ben Franklin's kite.

Ben Franklin's Lightning Mouth
EXPERIMENT 15

This experiment is a cool way of producing lightning (or a small-scale version of it) in your own mouth: But remember, the same forces are at work as the ones that produce real lightning. You'll be asked to crunch a Wint-O-Green Life Savers candy with your teeth. Sounds easy enough, but when you crunch the Life Saver, some electrons are sent out and they bump into nitrogen molecules in the air. This collision releases energy, which we see as light. The key to the experiment is the type of Life Saver, because not all will work. You also create sparks when you crunch fruit-flavored Life Savers, but those sparks are ultraviolet light, which our eyes cannot see. The oil of wintergreen is the chemical methyl salicylate, which absorbs the ultraviolet light and reemits the energy as blue-green visible light. The result is that neat flash of blue "lightning" in your mouth.

MATERIALS

- WINT-O-GREEN LIFE SAVERS CANDY
- FRIEND (TO ACT AS A WITNESS) OR MIRROR

TAKE CARE!

What advice would your parents give you after eating candy (even if it was in the cause of science)? That's right: Don't forget to brush your teeth afterward! Otherwise, you can figure on this being a pretty low-risk, high-reward experiment.

1. Turn off the lights and shut the curtains in a room to get it as dark as possible.

2. Wait about a minute to let your eyes adjust to the darkness.

3 Pop a Wint-O-Green Life Saver into your mouth and get a mirror or summon your friend.

4 Keeping your mouth open, close down hard on the Life Saver to make a crisp, clean break.

5 You should see some bright blue flashes as the candy breaks up: These come from static electricity.

EXPERIMENT 16

This experiment is a simple demonstration of what scientists would come to discover in the decades after Franklin's experimenting: that electricity and magnetic force are related. Both are based on opposite charges (think of north and south on a compass, which relates to the Earth's magnetic field). And just as you can find that opposite charges (electrical or magnetic) attract each other, you can also demonstrate how the same charges repel each other. This experiment takes a familiar demonstration and gives it a new twist.

The rule of "opposites attract and like repels like" applies to magnetic forces as well as electricity. In fact, scientists use the term electromagnetism to describe how the positive–negative relationship within magnetic fields affects the positive–negative relationship within electric fields—and vice versa. This explains why you can use a battery or other electrical source to build a magnet.

This experiment shows how "like repels like." You've probably rubbed a balloon against your hair or a wool sweater and then stuck it on a wall, which shows how the opposite charges of balloon and wall make them stick to each other. This experiment shows what happens to two of those rubbed balloons once they have the same charge. Just think—engineers have worked on the same principle to lift trains off electrically charged tracks!

MATERIALS

- 4-FOOT LENGTH OF STRING
- RULER
- 2 BALLOONS
- A FRIEND TO HELP YOU
- WOOL SWEATER

TAKE CARE!
It's hard to find anything remotely risky with this experiment, even though you're working with electrical forces throughout.

1 Tie the string to the middle of the ruler so you have 2 equal lengths of string hanging down from the knot.

2 Tie each balloon to an end of the string so that both balloons are hanging exactly next to each other about 2 feet under the ruler.

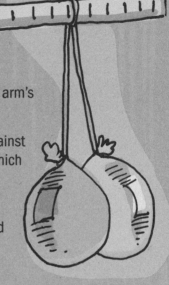

3 Have your friend hold the ruler at arm's length.

4 Rub one side of each balloon against a wool sweater, and remember which side of each has been rubbed.

5 Position the balloons so that the rubbed sides face each other and let go.

6 They should swing together then bounce back, and then swing together and bounce back . . . until the charge wears off.

Hey! Stop being so negative!

I'm not the only one who's negative around here. . .

Galvani's Circuit and
VOLTA'S BATTERY

...THE INSPIRATION FOR FRANKENSTEIN

Ben Franklin wasn't the only scientist to be fascinated by the mysterious power of electricity. But although Ben was willing to face catastrophe in testing his theories about electricity (see pages 89–93), his work never inspired anyone to write a horror story that would leave generations of readers terrified.

By comparison, the Italian scientist and doctor Luigi Galvani really did inspire one of the scariest creations in literature— Frankenstein's monster. Think of those famous Frankenstein movies, with the creature still lifeless in his creator's laboratory. And then, with a flick of a switch, sparks fly, an electric buzz fills the room . . . and the monster opens his eyes.

Working in his own lab in 1771, Luigi Galvani probably had no idea that his serious research would inspire Mary Shelley to write *Frankenstein* 45 years later. Like other scientists of his time, he was fascinated by Ben Franklin's study of electricity and curious about just what effect it had on the world around him. Many scientists—including Galvani—had a machine for generating static electricity. Such a device, called an Influence Machine, consisted of a sphere made of insulating material that could be turned with a crank and rubbed: The static charge that built up could then be drawn off.

Galvani's main work was the study of animal structure, and that day in 1771 he had been dissecting (taking apart for study) dead frogs. The static electricity machine was on in the background when Galvani touched a metal scalpel to the frog legs: They twitched and jumped! Galvani worked out that the metal scalpel had picked up an electrical charge, which had caused the frog legs to jump.

With this thought still in his head (and knowing that lightning was electrical), Galvani hung the frog legs outside his window during a thunderstorm. Sure enough, they began to twitch! But things got a little strange when the legs continued to twitch even after the storm had passed. Had the electricity in the lightning somehow brought the frog's legs back to life? Had the electricity somehow stayed inside the legs?

Galvani's discoveries captured the imagination of the world. "Creating" life or bringing people back

Luigi Galvani (1737–1798) vestigating why the dead frog's legs were twitching in a thunderstorm.

from the "dead" could lead to all sorts of potentially catastrophic horrors: a planet populated by the undead, for instance, or monsters like Frankenstein. Luckily Alessandro Volta, Galvani's friend and fellow scientist, did not buy into the mass hysteria at the time. In fact, he believed that Galvani's discoveries had opened a door that would revolutionize the world of science.

When Galvani first showed Volta his twitching frog legs, Volta did not agree that it was either the lightning or an electric current inside the frog legs that caused the movement. He believed the twitching was caused by the electric current produced by the various metals touching the frog: The scalpel Galvani used for dissection, and the brass hooks that held the frog's legs in place outside the window. These metals formed a "closed circuit" that was the key to the "twitching."

To prove it, Volta stacked a bunch of zinc and silver disks on top of one another, alternating zinc, silver, zinc, etc. In between every other zinc and silver disk, he placed a piece of cardboard that had been soaked in a salt solution. When a wire connecting the bottom zinc disk to the top silver disk produced sparks, it proved that an electric current had passed through the pile of metal and salt disks. Galvani was convinced—but even better, Volta had just produced the world's first battery!

THE SCIENCE BEHIND IT

LIKE SOME OTHER SCIENTISTS WHO HAVE PAVED the way for—or achieved—great breakthroughs, Luigi Galvani didn't know exactly what was going on in his famous frog leg experiments. So, we can say that he got it right and got it wrong at the same time. He was right in identifying electricity as the heart of the process.

But Galvani got it wrong by believing that all animals—dead or alive—were able to produce the electricity themselves. He believed that the twitching frog legs were examples of such "animal electricity." But after seeing Volta's demonstration, Galvani understood that it was the link between the metal and the electricity that caused the twitching.

Scientists now use the term "bioelectricity" to describe the relationship between electrical forces and living tissue. It normally involves animals receiving and reacting to—rather than producing—electrical currents. An electric current is simply a flow of negatively charged particles (electrons) through a substance toward positively charged particles. That was the concept behind Volta's battery, where metals and salt-water turned out to be excellent conductors, meaning they allowed electrons to pass through them easily. Some substances, like wood or rubber, don't allow

zinc

silver

salt solution

electrons to pass through. They are called insulators. Animals, it turns out, are excellent conductors, which is why Galvani's frog twitched. Very few animals can actually produce an electric charge, though. One exception is the electric eel (see box below). Another exception is the shark, which can pick up even tiny changes to the electrical field around it.

The **electric eel** is one animal that Galvani would have loved: It produces an electric shock for hunting and self-defense. How? The eel's brain sends signals to organs that contain electrolytes (electrically charged salts) arranged on more than 5,000 tiny plates. The signal triggers the release of positively charged sodium, which sends an electric current toward its prey or attacker.

Galvani's Hair-Raising
EXPERIMENT 17

This experiment is a "hair-raising" demonstration of human bioelectricity. By rubbing a balloon on your friend's hair, you are actually transferring some electrons from your friend's hair onto the balloon. This change to the flow of electrons causes an imbalance, leaving your friend's hair with a positive charge and the balloon with a negative. And they do say that opposites attract . . .

TAKE CARE!

This experiment works best if your volunteer has long hair that naturally flops down if she bends over. It still works—but far less obviously—if your volunteer has curly hair. Don't worry about getting a shock. This experiment is all about static electricity, which can't even go near danger levels with just a balloon and a head of hair.

MATERIALS

- A BALLOON, BLOWN UP AND TIED
- A LONG-HAIRED VOLUNTEER

1 Have the volunteer stand in the middle of the room so that your friends have a clear view.

2 Rub the balloon briskly back and forth on your friend's hair for about 10 to 15 seconds.

3 Slowly pull the balloon out and away from your friend's hair.

4 Her hair should stand on end, attracted to the balloon.

5 See how far you can pull the balloon away before it loses its power to attract hair.

Volta's Nickel-Penny Battery
EXPERIMENT 18

This experiment will enable you to make a battery using only some old coins. Nickels carry a slight positive charge and pennies carry a negative charge. Piling them together isn't enough to make them work as a battery, though, which is why you need the saltwater paper to act as an electrolyte (just as an electric eel uses sodium). The French word for battery is *pile*, which shows that the first batteries were made in this way.

MATERIALS

- MEASURING CUP
- DRINKING GLASS
- WATER
- SALT
- WOODEN SPOON
- PAPER TOWEL
- PENNIES
- SCISSORS
- NICKELS
- COPPER WIRE
- BLACK ELECTRICAL TAPE

TAKE CARE!

Make sure your pile of coins is secure. It's worth giving some thought beforehand to how you will tape the pile together. Some people rush that stage and wind up with a mess of coins and paper.

1 Pour ¼ cup water into the glass.

2 Add 1 teaspoon of salt and stir well with the wooden spoon.

3 Fold one piece of paper towel in half and then over on itself 3 more times so you have a long rectangle about 2 inches wide.

4 Lay a penny near one end of the paper towel and cut the towel just beyond the penny.

5 Keep the penny pinched on this small piece of folded paper towel and use it as a guide (or pattern) to trim the paper into a circle the same size as the coin.

6 Repeat step 5 until you run out of paper. You should wind up with 5 or 6 circles of folded paper.

7 Line up a row of nickels (as many as there are paper circles), keeping your pennies nearby.

8 Cut two 18-inch lengths of copper wire and tape the end of one of them to the first nickel, and then put the nickel back with the wire side down.

9 Dip a paper circle in the saltwater, squeeze out the drops, and put it on a nickel.

10 Repeat step 9 until each nickel in the line is covered.

11 Put a penny on each nickel-paper pile and then stack them on top of each other, taping the second bit of copper wire to the top penny.

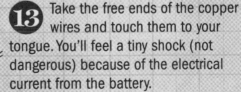

12 Cut several lengths of tape about 6 inches each and use them to wrap the pile together tightly, but leaving a bit of coin visible at each end.

13 Take the free ends of the copper wires and touch them to your tongue. You'll feel a tiny shock (not dangerous) because of the electrical current from the battery.

The Montgolfiers'
HOT-AIR BALLOON

BOLDLY GOING WHERE NO MAN HAS GONE BEFORE

O n June 4, 1783, a group of spectators gathered in the marketplace of Annonay, a small town in southern France. At the center of the town square stood a strange, globe-shaped object made of coarse cloth and stiff paper. A network of cords reinforced the outside of the globe and, looking closely, people could see some of the 1,800 buttons that held the pieces of fabric and paper together.

Joseph and Jacques Montgolfier, whose father owned a local paper mill, busied themselves around the cloth globe and began stoking a fire near the opening at the bottom of it. They announced that the *ballon* (French for "bag," and the origin of the English word *balloon*) would rise up into the heavens. Sure enough, as they added more wood to the fire, the balloon began to rise up off the ground. It continued to rise, and rise, and rise . . . until it was more than a mile above the astonished onlookers.

News of the Montgolfiers' balloon triumph spread across France like wildfire. The public was fascinated and fearful at the same time. Some local farmers saw the floating balloon and thought it was a monster. Other people wondered what would happen to human beings if they were to go on a balloon flight. Would the sudden climb into the sky hurt or even kill them? Could balloons be used in war?

Many people took the view that "If God wanted Man to fly, He would have given him wings." But the Montgolfiers were determined to try a human flight. First, they were invited to demonstrate their balloon to King Louis XVI at his palace in Versailles. On September 19, 1783, they sent a balloon carrying a sheep, a duck, and a rooster into the sky for eight minutes. They all survived, which added to the public demand for a human balloon flight.

Just over three weeks later, two volunteers, Pilâtre de Rozier and Marquis d'Arlandes, rose up in a balloon that remained tethered to the ground at Versailles. Then, on November 21, the same pair took off in the first "free flight" through the sky. They flew for about 25 minutes and landed more than five miles away, proving that the Montgolfier balloon was capable of human transport. Of course, flying in a basket under

The Montgolfier brothers, c. 1783.

a balloon filled with hot air does carry the potential for catastrophe. Only two years after becoming one of the world's first "aeronauts," de Rozier was killed when his hot-air balloon exploded in what became history's first balloon catastrophe. More would follow. A man named Jean-Pierre François Blanchard, who was one of the first aeronauts to fly across the English Channel, died in a balloon accident less than a decade later, and his wife, Madéleine-Sophie Blanchard, the world's first woman aeronaut, died less than 10 years after her husband in yet another horrific balloon catastrophe.

THE SCIENCE BEHIND IT

THE MONTGOLFIERS GOT THE TECHNOLOGY exactly right, but they were wide of the mark when it came to explaining the science. They believed that a burning fire produced a special gas (which they called "Montgolfier gas") that could cause objects to rise. In fact, the only gas that their balloons used was normal air.

Air is simply a mixture of gases, and when they are heated, gases expand. The Montgolfiers, like modern hot-air balloonists, heated the air inside the balloon using an open flame. Then a scientific principle known as the Ideal Gas Law comes into play. This law states that as a gas becomes warmer, the space between the gas molecules becomes greater; that means that the same amount of gas (in the case of these balloons, the gas is air) becomes less dense.

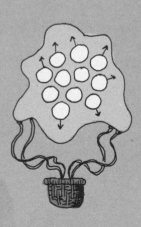

The eleven molecules inside this balloon are crowded together because they are at normal temperature. The air inside this balloon is dense.

When heated up, the space between the eleven molecule becomes greater, making the gas (the air) less dense.

And as the air becomes less dense, it expands and displaces some of the cooler, heavier air around it. That difference in weight is called the buoyant force, which increases as the balloon continues to inflate, but also fights against the downward force of gravity. Once the total weight of the displaced air is greater than that of the balloon, basket, and passengers, the balloon will start to rise.

A skilled balloonist knows when—and for how long—to warm up the air to get the right amount of lift. Of course, it is possible to pump a gas that is lighter than air into a balloon to get the same result. The floating balloons sold at fairgrounds are pumped full of helium.

The Montgolfier Hot-Air Trash Bag
EXPERIMENT 19

The centerpiece of this experiment is not, as you might expect, a fancy balloon but a humble trash bag. You fill it up with air and then let the Sun do its work. As the air is warmed up inside the trash bag, it starts to expand. But surely the Sun is also warming the air outside the bag, so they're both expanding at the same rate? Not quite true: The black of the trash bag absorbs more radiation (and heat), so the air inside gets that little bit warmer. Slowly but surely it rises up, along with its precious payload. There are two things to remember, though. The first is that you have the best chance of success by doing this on a sunny and calm summer's day. The second is that you must be patient: It could take an hour or more to reach liftoff.

MATERIALS

- 20-GALLON LIGHTWEIGHT (NOT HEAVY-DUTY) BLACK TRASH BAG WITH A TWIST TIE
- STRING
- A TOY SOLDIER OR TINY STUFFED ANIMAL
- HAIR DRYER (OPTIONAL)

TAKE CARE!

Remember that plastic bags are dangerous and can cause suffocation. Take great care using any bag, and never let a young child have it.

1 Hold the trash bag open with both hands and then whoosh it around until it nearly fills up with air.

W Hoosh!

2 Twist the top and seal it with string or a twist tie.

3 Tie a 6-foot length of string to the knotted end of the bag and then tie your toy soldier or stuffed animal to the string.

4 Just wait. Depending on how warm it is outside, the bag will start to rise and then float up, up, and away, with your "passenger." Don't let it float too far, though. Your neighbors might not want a black trash bag landing in their backyard—and it's certainly not good for the environment if it lands in a park or the ocean.

5 If you get impatient or simply run low on time, you can "fast forward" by taking the balloon inside and filling it with hot air from a hair dryer. Have someone hold the opening over the hair dryer, seal it up again when it's full, and take it back outside.

The Montgolfier Ping-Pong
EXPERIMENT 20

This experiment is a kind of slow-motion version of the Montgolfiers' triumphant technique to cause the air to expand inside a balloon. In this case, a Ping-Pong ball stands in for your "balloon," and warm water (instead of fire) is used to heat the air up inside your "balloon." As it warms and expands, the air exerts an outward force. You wouldn't be able to see this force at work with a normal Ping-Pong ball, though, which is why you use a dented ball for this experiment: The hot air inside the ball expands with enough force to push outward against the inside of the ball, popping it back into shape.

MATERIALS

TAKE CARE!
This works only on balls that are not pierced or cracked.

- SMALL MIXING BOWL

- HOT WATER (THE HOTTEST FROM THE FAUCET SHOULD DO)

- A DENTED PING-PONG BALL

- EMPTY PLASTIC DRINK BOTTLE (WITH LID OFF)

1 Fill the mixing bowl with hot water.

2 Drop the ball into the water.

3 Hold the plastic bottle upside down with the opening just touching the floating ball.

4 Carefully push the bottle down so the ball goes underwater.

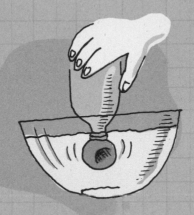

5 Keep the bottle and ball in place until the dent pops out (usually less than a minute).

Edward Jenner's
MIRACLE VACCINE

WILL WE ALL TURN INTO COWS?

Are you afraid of needles when you go to the doctor? Why—because you're worried that they might hurt? Or that you might turn into a cow?

A *what*? That's right—a cow. And that is what many people feared would happen if they allowed themselves to be jabbed with a needle when this practice was introduced more than 200 years ago. But the alternative was even worse—running the risk of dying from the killer disease smallpox.

People in the 18th century dreaded the disease smallpox, which is a deadlier version of chicken pox. Up to 60 percent of people who became infected with it went on to die from the disease; some experts estimate that 400,000 Europeans died from smallpox each year in the 1700s. Those who survived were often left with ugly scars all over their bodies. Many people lost hope that a smallpox treatment would ever be found.

English surgeon Edward Jenner (1749–1823) was one medical expert who never gave up hope that a cure for smallpox could be developed. He was open to all sorts of ideas in his search for a cure, so when he heard that milkmaids who picked up cowpox (a mild disease) from the cows they milked seemed to develop an immunity to smallpox, he was intrigued. Those milkmaids, Jenner noted, developed blisters on their hands from the cowpox, so he figured that the pus inside these blisters must be the key to the immunity against smallpox. But how could he be sure? His hypothesis would have to be tested.

In 1796, Jenner took some fluid and pus from the blisters of a young milkmaid named Sarah Nelmes, who had contracted cowpox. Then, over the course of several days, he injected some of this pus into the arm of an eight-year-old boy named James Phipps. James developed a slight headache and felt a little chilly (he had actually contracted a mild case of cowpox), but soon recovered. Then Jenner performed the really terrifying experiment: He injected James with pus from a smallpox blister. James did not become sick. Jenner tried it again,

The word **vaccine** (derived from *vacca*, Latin for "cow") refers back to that first experiment by Edward Jenner.

but once more James showed no signs of developing smallpox.

Jenner's experiment on James Phipps was the first example of vaccination as a way of preventing disease. Because of this, and the ability to apply the same principle to developing vaccines to other diseases, such as typhus and rabies, Jenner is credited with saving more lives than any other person who has ever lived.

Now, you say, what could be considered even remotely potentially catastrophic about this brilliant scientific advancement? Well, the same science that caused immunologists to successfully create vaccines for some of mankind's most horrific diseases also led them to understand enough about the viruses themselves to contain them, keep them, and even weaponize them. For example, in 1940, the Imperial Japanese Army Air Force dropped bombs on China loaded with bubonic plague–carrying fleas. Other countries had their own versions of this "biological warfare," but in 1975 22 nations signed the Biological and Toxic Weapons Convention, which banned the use of biological agents in weapons.

An illustration of Edward Jenner vaccinating James Phipps. If the vaccine had not worked, the boy would have developed smallpox after Jenner injected him with the disease. Talk about potentially catastrophic!

THE SCIENCE BEHIND IT

EDWARD JENNER WAS A PIONEER IN FIGHTING DIS-
ease, but he was the first to admit that much older
practices and bits of knowledge helped him develop
that first vaccine he used on young James Phipps.

For thousands of years, people had observed that
someone rarely contracted a deadly disease if they
had already survived it once. Eight centuries before
Jenner, Chinese people made powder from smallpox scabs and blew it up the noses of healthy people.
This form of introducing a version of a disease into
a person to prevent the real version from developing is called inoculation. Most people would develop
a weaker version of smallpox and then never suffer
from the full-strength version.

Jenner's vaccination was a safer version. Rather than
using the same disease, it used a nondeadly alternative. Modern vaccinations against viral diseases such
as polio and measles use disease particles that have
been weakened or killed. Vaccines against bacterial
diseases (such as cholera and tuberculosis) use an
inactive portion of the disease bacteria.

The underlying science for inoculation and vaccination is the same. The body's immune system (its
defense against diseases) reacts to a disease by producing antibodies. These are special proteins that
help the white blood cells identify and destroy dangerous invaders. When a person develops smallpox
or measles, the body might not produce enough antibodies fast enough to ward off the disease. A vaccine
sends the same signal to the immune system as the

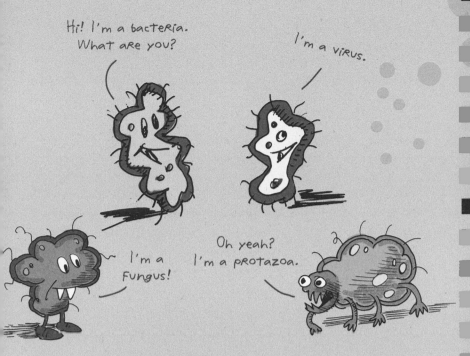

actual disease itself, so the body starts producing those wonderful antibodies without having to fight off the full effects of the disease at the same time.

Diseases are now known to be caused by microorganisms that are called "germs." This rather unscientific term covers a wide range of microorganisms, including bacteria, viruses, fungi (related to mushrooms), and protozoa (tiny animals). Although they are as different from each other as oak trees are from hornets, they all have the capacity to attack and weaken our bodies in one way or another, causing diseases. And of course, the other thing they share is their tiny size, too small for the naked eye to see. That is why the invention of the microscope was so important. Microscopes use the ability of a curved lens to bend—or refract—light as it passes through. The refracted light magnifies, or enlarges, the image we see, enabling us to see many of those tiny germs.

Edward Jenner's Water Microscope

EXPERIMENT 21

This experiment helps you develop your own microscope so you can catch a glimpse of this "hidden world" that is on the front line of medicine. The drop of water you're using in this experiment actually acts like a lens that magnifies what is seen through it because of refraction. Light travels more slowly through water than air, so when it moves from one to the other it bends (refracts), causing the image in the center to appear bigger.

MATERIALS

- WATER FROM A PUDDLE OR A POND
- SAUCER
- AN EMPTY, CLEAR PLASTIC SODA BOTTLE
- SCISSORS
- CLEAN WATER
- SPOON

TAKE CARE!
Sometimes it takes a couple of tries to get the right-shaped drop. Keep trying—it will work out!

1 Collect some dirty water from a puddle, drainpipe, or pond and pour it onto the saucer.

2 Set the saucer down on a table or counter.

3 Cut a strip of clear plastic—about 2 inches long and 1 inch wide—from the side of the plastic bottle. Set the plastic strip down near the saucer.

4 Run the cold-water faucet slowly over the handle of the spoon.

5 Move the spoon over the plastic strip and dab a drop of water onto the center of the plastic. (The drop of water should be about ¼ inch wide.)

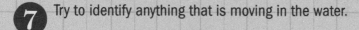

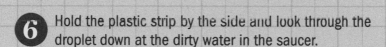

6 Hold the plastic strip by the side and look through the droplet down at the dirty water in the saucer.

7 Try to identify anything that is moving in the water.

Edward Jenner's Germ
EXPERIMENT 22

This experiment shows how simply touching an infected person can spread diseases very quickly—something we have all heard in those warnings about seasonal flu. Basically, you're using glitter to represent the spread of germs on your hand: Each dot of glitter represents a microbe. By "infecting" yourself with glitter, then shaking hands with another person and having that person shake hands with another (and so on and so forth) you can actually see the spread of the disease as it makes its way around a room. If this experiment doesn't teach you the importance of washing your hands, then nothing will.

MATERIALS

- A PLATE OR LARGE SALAD BOWL

- BODY GLITTER (ENOUGH TO FORM A ¼-INCH LAYER ON THE PLATE)

- 20 OR MORE VOLUNTEERS

- FLASHLIGHT (OPTIONAL)

TAKE CARE!

Make sure you leave enough time for people to wash the glitter off their hands. Lots of soapy water usually does the trick. And even if people don't have glitter on their hands, they should still wash their hands after this experiment: Real germs are a lot "stickier" than glitter and a lot harder to shake off.

1 Make sure all the volunteers wash their hands (this sets the "medical" tone, plus clean hands make it easier to see the effects of the experiment).

2 Spread a ¼-inch layer of glitter evenly on the plate.

3 Set the plate on a counter, desk, or table and have a volunteer rub his or her right hand in it.

4 Have the volunteer shake hands with another volunteer. The first volunteer (the "infected person") can stand aside.

5 Have the second volunteer shake hands with someone else, and then everyone (except the first volunteer) should move around the room, shaking hands with others.

6 Continue for 3 minutes—there's no need for people to keep absolute count of whose hand they've shaken.

7 Go around the room to see how many people have glitter on their hands: How many have become "infected"? (Sometimes you can pick up a "hidden" piece of glitter by shining a flashlight on a person's hand.)

AUDAX AEREOS GAUDET TENTAREVOLA

M: GARNERIN.

Garnerin's
PARACHUTE

DEFYING GRAVITY—SORT OF

The Montgolfier brothers stirred people's imagination by organizing those heroic balloon ascents (see pages 109–113). Within a few years, balloonists were taking to the skies all over Europe. For some people—either floating above the earth or simply looking up—balloons were poetry in motion, moving gently this way and that, guided by the slightest breeze. Others, however, saw balloons as a stepping-stone to even wilder assaults on the law of gravity.

And just what would be more daring than being let loose into the sky in a world without airports, radar, or radio controls? Isn't going up in a balloon risky enough? Well, there's one thing you could do that might be a lot scarier: Jump out of a balloon!

That is where we pick up the story of André-Jacques Garnerin (1769–1823), a French scientist and soldier who had always been interested in flight. As a young man, he had studied the Montgolfier balloons as well as some of the first attempts to produce parachutes. Those early parachutes, also produced by French inventors, were based on the design of an umbrella, with spokes running out from the center.

A technical drawing of Garnerin's parachute design.

Garnerin felt that such designs could be developed to produce a parachute that could carry an adult safely to the ground from thousands of feet up. He had several years to work on his plan while he was a prisoner of war in Hungary during the early 1790s. At one point he even hoped to produce a parachute that he could use to escape from the castle where he was held prisoner.

After he was freed and moved back to France, Garnerin went on to produce a large parachute made from silk that had no rigid frame. Borrowing a bit of know-how from his countryman Jean-Pierre

François Blanchard (see page 111), Garnerin made a parachute that was 23 feet wide and resembled a closed umbrella when shut. On October 22, 1797, Garnerin demonstrated this parachute at Parc Monceau in Paris. Sitting in a basket at the base of the parachute, which was tied to a hot-air balloon, Garnerin rose 3,000 feet in the air in the balloon before cutting the rope that attached the basket to the balloon. The basket, with Garnerin in it, floated slowly down to the ground, and when Garnerin walked safely from the basket, the crowd that had witnessed his death-defying exploit broke into thunderous applause.

For the next 15 years or so, Garnerin and his wife, Jeanne-Geneviève, demonstrated their parachuting skills all over France and in England. But the potential for catastrophe was always there, of course—though sometimes catastrophe strikes differently than we imagine. Did Garnerin die from a speeding plunge to the earth when a faulty parachute failed to open? Not quite. He died when he was struck by a beam while making a balloon in Paris.

THE SCIENCE BEHIND IT

PARACHUTES WORK BECAUSE THEY USE A PRINCIPLE called air resistance to slow their fall. The term "air resistance" helps to explain this process pretty well on its own, since it paints a picture of air having the strength to resist—try to block—something else. And in this case, the "something else" is a falling object.

Without air resistance, everything would fall to the ground at the same rate. So if you held a feather in one hand and a pebble in the other and let go, they would land at the same time.

But you wouldn't really expect that to happen in real life. You know that the feather would fall very slowly, rocking back and forth and getting whisked along by any puff of wind as it floated down. That is because it is affected by air resistance.

Air, like everything else, is made up of the tiny building blocks called molecules. Something that is falling has to pass through these air molecules. A pebble or a baseball, pencil, or egg can pass through the air quickly because they simply push aside the molecules and find their way through. These objects are much denser than air, which means they have more matter (and therefore molecules) packed into the same space as air.

A feather is much less dense, and in fact not much denser than air. Its mass is spread across quite a large space. That makes it harder for the feather to push aside the air molecules. Scientists such as Garnerin understood air resistance and could see it on display whenever a gust of wind blew up beneath an umbrella. The umbrella could not resist the gust of wind easily, and whoever was holding it would feel it being tugged by the wind.

ROCK

FEATHER

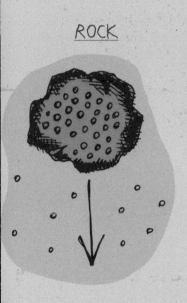

The molecules inside the Rock are denser than the molecules outside the Rock.

The molecules inside the Feather are less dense than the molecules outside the Feather.

Those same scientists worked out that the same principles of air resistance would work in reverse. That is, an umbrella (like a feather) would float down because its mass was spread across a wide area. And if one or two umbrellas linked together could keep a cat safe when dropped from a tree (one of the first French experiments), then an even bigger umbrella —a parachute—should do the same for a human being.

Garnerin's Parachute
EXPERIMENT 23

This experiment gives you a chance to play around with your understanding of air resistance. Like Garnerin, you can check out how much air a parachute of a certain size displaces. The recommended size of cut-out trash bag is about right to help an egg float down safely. If you're very curious (and don't mind possibly breaking a few eggs along the way), you can test the results with a smaller piece bag—to see how small you can go while still saving the egg. Or you could "go big" and try parachutes a little bit bigger, timing each descent and comparing.

MATERIALS

- FULL-SIZE TRASH BAG
- SCISSORS
- PENCIL
- PLASTIC CUP
- KITE STRING
- 3 OR 4 EGGS

TAKE CARE!
Make sure no one is standing right beneath you when you drop the parachute. And just *in case* the egg breaks, make sure you do the experiment far from anything that could get damaged or ruined by a broken egg.

1 Cut a large square (each side about 2 feet) from the trash bag.

2 Use the pencil to make 4 tiny holes 2 inches in from each corner of the square. Also make 3 tiny holes in the center of the square. These will provide stability and allow a little air to escape through the top of the parachute. (Real parachutes have these center holes to stop them from behaving like kites and getting pushed upward by sudden gusts of wind.)

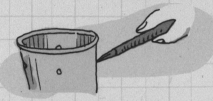

3 Carefully make 4 tiny holes in the plastic cup, about an inch from the top and evenly spaced around the cup.

4 Cut 4 lengths of kite string, each 2 feet long.

5 Carefully tie one end of each string to the cup, making the knot inside the cup so the string doesn't pass back through.

6 Tie the other end of each piece of string to one of the 4 holes in the corners of the square. You should now have what looks kind of like a parachute.

7 Hold the parachute by the center where you made the holes and put an egg in the cup.

8 Carry the loaded parachute to an upstairs window, hold your arm out, and release the parachute. It should fall safely to the ground without breaking the egg.

9 If you really get the hang of it, try to get your friends to make their own parachutes and then have a competition to see whose parachute takes longest to fall from the same height.

George Stephenson's
STEAM TRAIN

BREAKING THE SPEED LIMIT AT 14 MPH!

Most of us have ridden on—or at least seen—trains making their way from city to city. In many parts of the world, including the Boston–Washington "corridor," where lots of big cities are close to each other, taking the train can be even quicker than flying from one city to another. Some trains in France and Japan regularly reach speeds of more than 200 mph.

So it might come as a surprise to learn that many people (including scientists) believed that the first trains were death traps. Why? Because they would be transporting human beings faster than they had ever traveled, and the human body was not built to withstand hair-raising speeds of 14 mph, or even more!

Many inventors in the late 1700s and early 1800s began experimenting with ways to use "steam" to power movement. Boilers, which were closed vessels in which water was heated, were already in use by then, and boiler technology had reached a level where the safe production of high-pressure steam was possible. It was a natural next step to figure out how to harness steam power to propel carts and wagons along tracks. In 1794 a man named William Murdoch was the first to develop a model steam carriage based on the principle of "strong steam." His neighbor, Richard Trevithick, then used those ideas to create the first steam engine. Others followed suit, as these first railroads were perfect for transporting coal and other loads in Great Britain, which led the world in industrial matters. It took George Stephenson, though, to turn the coal-carrying steam engines into passenger-carrying vehicles. After working his way up from a poor background in a coal-mining village, Stephenson had studied engineering in his spare time. He produced a train that could haul 30 tons of coal uphill at 4 mph in 1814, which was quite a feat. But what he really wanted was to build a train that would transport people.

Great Britain at the time of Stephenson's train was well into a period of fast-paced change called the **Industrial Revolution**. The word **industrial** refers to the manufacture of products. **Revolution** usually means a sudden departure from the way things used to be. In the case of the Industrial Revolution, which began in Great Britain in the late 1700s and then spread to other countries, a series of inventions and new working practices took hold. Most of these developments involved the widespread use of machinery, producing goods on a vast scale.

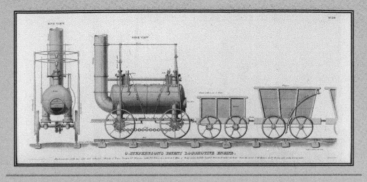

George Stephenson's design for the steam locomotive and railroad cars.

Now, the public at the time was wary of anything that promised too much speed. An early railway locomotive, Brunton's Mechanical Traveller—also known as the Steam Horse—had killed 16 spectators when its boiler exploded in County Durham, England, in 1815. And aside from the danger of explosions, it was commonly thought that passengers' bodies would not stand the speed and that horses and cattle near train lines would die of fright if a steam engine went by too fast. This, and the very distinct possibility that a boiler would explode or fires break out along train lines because of the coal burned to produce the steam, caused many people to think of steam engines as potentially catastrophic.

Despite these public concerns, Stephenson pushed ahead with his plans to demonstrate a passenger train in action. His chance came

Locomotion: the power or ability to move from place to place.

on September 27, 1825, when Stephenson himself took the controls of the *Locomotion* (as he named the locomotive) and its 80-ton load of coal on a 9-mile trip in just over two hours. More important, the train reached speeds of up to 24 mph—and included a car called "The Experiment," which carried six local men. Needless to say, none of the men suffered any side effects at the end of the ride.

THE SCIENCE BEHIND IT

STEPHENSON'S STEAM TRAIN WAS A WONDERFUL combination of science and engineering. The science is pretty easy to understand. When water is heated up to boiling point, it turns to steam and increases its pressure—it is pushing out in all directions. That extra pressure is the scientific core of the process, and how to direct that pressure is where the engineering comes into the picture.

Early Steam Engine

Chimney

Cylinders

Boiler

Fire Door

Coal

Fire Box

Water

Wheels

A steam train like Stephenson's must have THREE main elements: a boiler, cylinders, and driving wheels. The water is stored in a tank inside the boiler, and it's heated to a boil by a fire box, which is adjacent to the tank. A series of hollow metal tubes running through the boiler from the fire box to the chimney also helps bring the water to boil. A separate cart stores the coal, which is the fuel used to keep the fire in the fire box going. You may have seen old movies where a worker shovels coal into the fire box; it all had to be done by hand. Someone actually had to stand in the cart while it was moving and shovel the coal into the fire box in order to keep the water at a boil and make the steam. It's all about the steam in a steam engine, after all. That's what causes everything to move. The high-pressure steam would flow into the cylinders, causing the pistons inside the cylinders (pistons are like pieces of cork fitting snugly inside a bottle of wine) to go up and down. The pistons are attached to long rods that are connected to the wheels, and it's the up-and-down motion of the pistons that makes the wheels spin. After the steam has pushed through the cylinders, it escapes through a chimney. That's what causes the "chug-chug-chug" sound of the steam train: It's the used-up steam escaping through the chimney.

Stephenson's Steam Can

EXPERIMENT 24

Lots of interesting experiments demonstrate how air expands when it is heated up. In this experiment, you will be heating up a small amount of water in a can until it boils. The tablespoon of water turns into steam, which drives the air out of the can. You'll then plunge the can into cold water, which will send the temperature plummeting so that the steam will turn back into liquid water. This process is called condensation, and it refers to the change that happens to a gas (in this case, steam) when it cools to become a liquid, which is denser than the gas. But turning back to liquid means that the water takes up far less space, and as all of the air was driven out earlier, there's nothing to stop the pressure of the saucepan water pushing in on the can, which is why it gets crushed by the surrounding water.

MATERIALS

- STOVE
- FRYING PAN
- LARGE SAUCEPAN
- WATER
- TABLESPOON
- EMPTY SODA CAN
- OVEN MITT OR TONGS

TAKE CARE!
Because of the stove, hot pan, and boiling water, this experiment must be carried out by an adult.

1 Heat the frying pan on the stove until it is hot enough to use for cooking.

2 Meanwhile, pour cold water into the saucepan to a depth of about 1½ inches.

3 Carefully pour a tablespoon of water into the soda can.

4 Use the mitt or tongs to place the soda can on the frying pan. Listen for the bubbling sound of the water coming to a boil.

5 Leave the soda can there for another minute and then use the mitts or tongs to transfer it to the saucepan.

6 Place the soda can in the saucepan upside down, taking care that you don't get hit by any stray drops of hot water dripping from the can.

7 The soda can should collapse rapidly with a loud crunch.

Otis's Elevator
SAFETY BRAKE

FIGHTING CLAUSTROPHOBIA *AND* FEAR OF FALLING . . .

The Crystal Palace Exposition, held in a massive glass-walled building in Bryant Park from 1853 to 1854, was New York City's first World's Fair. More than a million people visited the huge exhibition center, which showcased the latest inventions, fashions, and must-have products. It is not surprising that the greatest showman of them all, P. T. Barnum, would find it an ideal spot to attract people to his Traveling World's Fair.

Barnum was particularly keen to publicize the work of a mechanical engineer, the founder of the Union Elevator and General

Machine Works Company. Elisha G. Otis, a farmer's son from Vermont who had moved to New York, arrived at the Exposition with an invention that would revolutionize the look of his adopted city. Even Mr. Barnum, who loved to exaggerate, underestimated just what Otis had to demonstrate—and where it would lead.

Otis climbed onto a platform that had ropes leading up to a system of pulleys. When Otis gave a signal, his assistants pulled down on the other end of the ropes, and the platform (really an open-sided elevator) began to climb. There was nothing too unusual in that: Factories and warehouses used similar hoists to lift goods between floors.

The elevator kept climbing, until Otis was more than 60 feet above the audience. Then he calmly reached down, picked up a long knife from a pillow by his feet, and began sawing back and forth on the rope holding his elevator car. The audience gasped as he continued to cut the rope until—*snap*—it was severed and the elevator started to fall. The crowd shrieked in horror but then was silenced, as the platform had stopped its fall and locked into place.

"All safe, ladies and gentlemen. All safe." Otis had just demonstrated—in the most dramatic

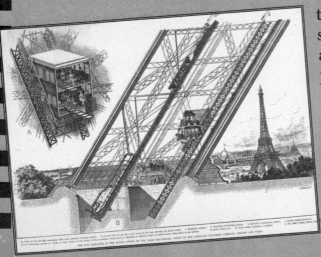

Otis's elevator brake at work in the Eiffel Tower.

way imaginable—the elevator safety brake. Elevators themselves had been around for decades, and Otis himself had worked in a warehouse that used an elevator to raise and lower beds several stories. But because the ropes holding those elevators would sometimes just break, sending the elevator plummeting—along with its cargo—they were always considered potentially catastrophic. No one could imagine human beings relying on these unpredictable bits of machinery.

Otis's invention provided just the sort of security that architects needed to build higher and higher. No more would they be limited by the numbers of staircases— or by elevators that kept dropping like stones. Thanks to Elisha Otis, the Age of the Skyscraper had dawned.

Although originally a nautical term, the word **skyscraper** was first used to define the tall buildings being built in New York City and Chicago in the late 1800s.

THE SCIENCE BEHIND IT

IF YOU LOOK CLOSELY NEXT TIME YOU'RE IN A TALL building, you might see the words "Otis Elevators" as you make your way up or down. Many people believe that Elisha Otis actually invented the elevator, but that is not the case. Elevators had been around for as long as people had been able to use ropes and pulleys to lift and lower weights that were too heavy to carry otherwise.

The ancient Roman architect Vitruvius, who lived about 2,000 years ago, wrote that the Greek inventor Archimedes had invented the elevator in the third century B.C. And King Louis XV was said to have a "Flying Chair" hanging in his chimney that would be pulled up or down by waiting servants. Pulleys, hoists, ropes, and cables had been put to work for centuries before Otis came on the scene.

But Otis's arrival was particularly special. New construction techniques had enabled people to build elevators that carried heavier loads even higher. These new elevators had perfected the use of a counterweight, a weight that balances the load by hanging down on the other side of the pulley. It weighed about the same as the elevator when it was half-full, making it easier to lift it.

You can see the same principle at work when you sit on a seesaw: Having someone on one side makes it easier to lift the person on the other side. If you have a 300-pound person on one side and a 30-pound person on the other, you know that they're not evenly balanced and the lighter person will always end up in the air.

So the mechanics behind the ups and downs of the elevator were clearly known by the time Otis made his famous demonstration for Barnum, but how did he come upon the great innovation of the brake? This had been the most potentially catastrophic part of the elevator before his time. What Otis did was to install a row of deep metal notches along the side of the elevator shaft. The elevator car was equipped with a set of teeth, or gears, that could spring out and lodge inside the notches, bringing the car to a halt.

Usually—when the car was going up or going down slowly—those safety teeth were drawn in. But if the car began to descend past a certain speed, a spring would release the teeth and lock the elevator car in place.

The Otis Elevator Company became enormously successful after the famous 1854 demonstration. Otis died from a sudden illness in 1861, too soon to see how his invention would change the face of modern cities. His legacy lives on, though, with more than 1.8 million Otis elevators going up and down all over the world.

Otis's Bobbin Elevator
EXPERIMENT 25

In this experiment, you'll get a chance to use your ingenuity to build an elevator using materials that are easy to find in the house—especially if someone in your family likes to sew. Used-up (empty) spools of thread, also known as bobbins, play the role of pulleys, and ordinary string does the work that strong steel cables do in life-size elevators.

This elevator will use many of the same principles as those in the Empire State Building and other famous skyscrapers, right down to the counterweight (in this case, a key). If you're really imaginative, you can put a small plastic figure on your elevator and re-create Elisha Otis's famous demonstration of 1854: But first you'll have to build a safety brake!

MATERIALS

- 1 PIECE OF PLYWOOD (ABOUT 2 FEET X 3 FEET)

- 6 EMPTY THREAD BOBBINS (THE SORT THAT ONCE HAD THREAD WOUND AROUND THEM)

- 6 NAILS (LONGER THAN A BOBBIN BUT NARROW ENOUGH TO FIT THROUGH THE HOLE IN THE BOBBIN)

- SHOEBOX

- HAMMER

- STRING

- SCISSORS

- HEAVY KEY (TO ACT AS A COUNTERWEIGHT)

TAKE CARE!

It's best to do the hammering part of this experiment on the ground outside. Remember also that you can tinker with the strings, nails, and bobbins until you get a good fit—just be patient.

Remember that the completed elevator will be attached to the plywood, which you will lean against a wall until it is as upright as you can get it (with one of the narrow sides resting on the ground).

1 Set the piece of plywood on the floor and nail 4 bobbins in an evenly spaced row running about 3 inches down from the top of the plywood (one of the narrow edges). The first (which you can call 1) should be about 6 inches in from the left-hand edge, and the others (2, 3, and 4) should be about 4 inches apart from each other.

2 Nail the other 2 bobbins (numbers 5 and 6) about 3 inches up from the bottom edge, so that they align with numbers 1 and 2.

3 Don't hammer the nails completely in: You want each bobbin to be able to spin.

4 Make 2 small holes, about an inch apart, in the two long sides of the shoebox. This will be your elevator car.

5 Rest the elevator car, with its open side up, on the plywood halfway between the 2 rows of spindles.

6 Cut a piece of string about 5 feet long and feed one end through the holes on the bottom of the elevator car and secure with a knot. This will be your "floor string."

7 Now cut 2 more pieces of string (2 feet and 3 feet) and run these through the holes in the top of the elevator car, securing with a knot. These will be your "ceiling strings."

8 Pass the "floor string" under bobbins 6 and 5, and then up to bobbin 1 (looping over it twice), then over bobbin 2.

9 Tie that "floor string" to the shorter of the 2 "ceiling strings."

10 Run the longer "ceiling string" up and over bobbins 3 and 4 and then about halfway down. Cut any excess string and attach the key to the end of this string.

11 All the strings should be taut and the bobbins should be able to spin beneath them. Make any adjustments.

12 Set the plywood upright and work the elevator by twisting bobbin 1 back and forth.

Darwin's Revolutionary
EVOLUTIONARY BOOK

ONE SMALL STEP FOR APE . . .

G reat Britain in the late 1850s was the most powerful country in the world. It had just emerged victorious from the Crimean War and was at peace. Its empire, on which it was said "the Sun never set" because it was so vast, was at its height. British factories led the world in many areas of industry, and its shipping fleet commanded the high seas while sending British goods to the four corners of the world.

This picture of peaceful might was shattered in 1859 by, of all things, a book. The author was no wild revolutionary calling for workers' rights or the death

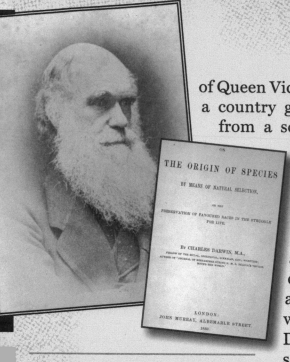

of Queen Victoria. Instead, he was a country gentleman who came from a social group that valued cricket and tea parties more than public outrage.

That man's name was Charles Darwin, and his work has continued to shape—and shake up—the wider world. In 1859, Darwin published a scientific work entitled *On the Origin of Species*. This book was the result of decades of research that Darwin

Charles Darwin was the author of *On the Origin of Species*, the book that changed the way many people viewed the human race. It was first published in 1859.

had conducted both in Britain and in travels across South America and the Pacific Islands. In it, Darwin introduced his theory that plants and animals need to evolve, or change, over the course of generations in order to adapt to their environment. They do this through a process called natural selection, which means that only those organisms best adapted to their environment will survive, and these plants and animals pass on their genes to future generations, thereby ensuring the survival of the species.

When *On the Origin of Species* was published, it caused quite a stir—one that hadn't been seen in the world since Galileo (see pages 69–73) tried to convince everyone that the Earth was not the center of the universe. And as with Galileo, the main opposition to Darwin was the church (in Darwin's case, it was the Church of England, not the Vatican). Many members of the Church of England believed in the literal truth of the Bible as an explanation for everything. For these believers, God created everything in the course of a week—including Man.

Some religious writers had used the Bible to find the age of the Earth itself. Many in the Church of England agreed with Bishop Ussher's calculation in the 17th century. He worked out that the first day of creation began on Sunday, October 23, 4004 B.C. The idea that the Earth might be millions—and even billions—of years old was an idea with potentially catastrophic consequences to people who believed in Ussher's calculations. If Darwin's theory of evolution proved the Bible wrong on the age of the Earth, what else could be proven wrong?

THE SCIENCE BEHIND IT

THE KEY TO DARWIN'S WORK WAS ACTUALLY IN its title—its full title, which most people never bothered to read: *On the Origin of Species by Means of Natural Selection, or the Preservation of Favoured Races in the Struggle for Life.* The key words in that mouthful are "natural selection." This idea is sometimes boiled down to a simple phrase: survival of the fittest. A healthy and strong plant or animal will have a better chance of reproducing (or being "preserved") than a weaker, unhealthy one. You can imagine, for example, a healthy male lion breeding with different lionesses while the weaker males in the group might never breed at all during their lives. Many of the qualities—later scientists would call them "genes"— of the healthy lion would be preserved in the next generation, and so on.

The lion example is one that we can easily imagine. Where Darwin was different was in how he patiently examined all sorts of species—moths, finches, pigeons—to see whether and how their populations evolved. He even spent eight years studying the evolution of barnacles!

Sometimes the reason for this survival was a bit random. For example, the earliest giraffes had to compete with other animals for the juiciest leaves. A mutation (an unexpected change in the genes) might give one giraffe a longer neck than other giraffes. This advantage would make that giraffe better able to survive—and to pass on the "mistaken" genes for long necks. Over time, those giraffes with the longest necks would be the "strongest" or the "fittest" to reproduce, and short-necked giraffes would not pass on their genes.

Of course, Darwin ran into big trouble when his readers concluded that human beings were also part of this process, and that modern man was a descendant of apes and even more primitive mammals that lived millions of years ago.

Darwin didn't just dream up his ideas. He based them on evidence of living and dead organisms. Some of the oldest evidence came from fossils, once-living organisms that have hardened over many years. Organisms fossilize (become fossils) in many stages. The first is when their soft tissue is eaten by scavengers and the remainder decomposes. Animals that are made up only of soft tissues—such as worms— never become fossils because all trace of them disappears at this point. What's left of other organisms— hard material such as teeth, horns, and bones—gets covered by layers of soil and sand. These layers protect the hard materials from wind and rain, causing them to decay very slowly. Meanwhile, water seeps through this underground area, and minerals within this water are absorbed by the hard "leftovers" of the organism through a process called osmosis. The new rocklike minerals (such as calcium and silica) replace the original chemicals, creating a hard replica, or fossil.

Osmosis: a chemical process in which molecules of a solution pass through a layer of material to reach a stronger concentration of that solution on the other side of the layer.

Darwin's Fossil
EXPERIMENT 26

This experiment allows you to speed up the process of fossil-making by a few million years, give or take a century. In fact, you'll be making a fossil in a week.

The secret is the sponge you'll be using. Sponges, as we all know, absorb a great deal of water. You'll be fossilizing a sponge by adding a salty concoction that will seep through the sand you've placed over the sponge, then be strained through the sponge on its way down before being sucked back up from the tray by osmosis. Then it evaporates, only to be topped off every day by you. Each time the water evaporates, it leaves some of the salts that had been in solution with the water. Each "dose of salts" hardens the fossil a bit more, until it really does look 40 million years old.

MATERIALS

- SCISSORS
- BATH SPONGE
- EMPTY PLASTIC 16-OUNCE MARGARINE TUB
- SMALL BAKING TRAY
- FINE SAND (SANDBOX SAND WORKS WELL)
- TABLESPOON
- WARM WATER
- PACK OF BATH SALTS
- CUP

TAKE CARE!

If your fossil still feels a little pliable, leave it to dry for another day.

1 Use the scissors to cut the sponge into a 3-dimensional shape. This shape will become your "fossil," so it could be in the shape of a dinosaur bone or tooth, or maybe even a primitive shellfish. Make sure the finished product can fit easily into the empty tub of margarine.

2 With the scissors, make a few small holes in the bottom of the margarine tub and rest it on the baking tray.

3 Fill the margarine tub with a 1-inch layer of sand, and then lay your sponge "fossil" on it.

4 Cover this with another ½-inch layer of sand.

5 Mix 4 tablespoons of warm water with 4 tablespoons of bath salts in the cup. Make sure the water is warm enough to dissolve the bath salts. Pour this mixture over the sandy tub, letting the liquid sink through the sand.

6 Leave the tub on a sunny windowsill for 5 days.

7 Repeat step 5 for each of those days.

8 Leave the tub without adding any more liquid for another 2 days.

9 Carefully remove your fossil, which should be very hard by now.

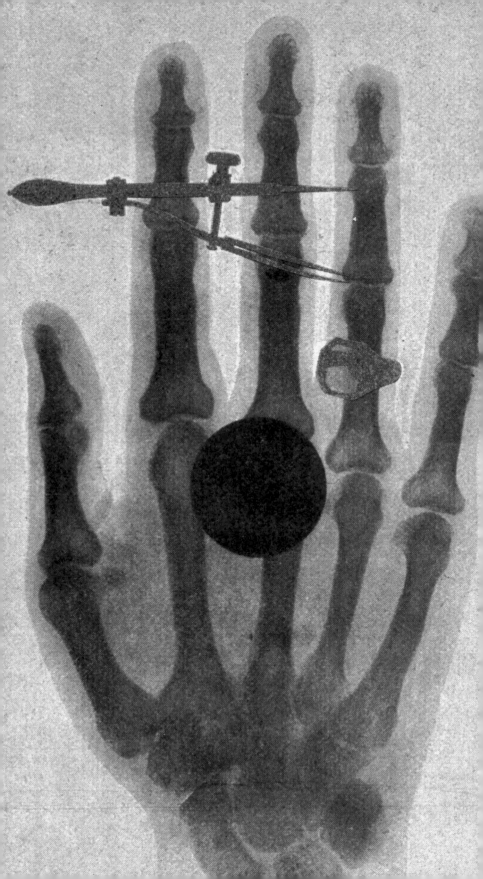

Röntgen Identifies
X-RAYS

"I HAVE SEEN MY DEATH!"

If anyone looked like our image of the wild-eyed scientist, it was the German physicist Wilhelm Conrad Röntgen. One of the most famous photographs of Röntgen shows his tall figure stooped over a table in his lab. The lamp held in his left hand casts spooky shadows across his dark brow and bushy beard. Here is a man, the photograph seems to say, who probably went to college with Dr. Frankenstein and whose own handmade monster didn't quite make it to the photograph.

In fact, Röntgen was a devoted husband and generous man who insisted that all of his medical discoveries be widely available to the public. He even donated the money from his 1901 Nobel Prize for Physics to his university. But that's jumping ahead of the story of how he got his wife to foresee her death.

Wilhelm Röntgen at work in his lab.

The story really begins in 1895, as Röntgen was working in his lab. The late 1800s was a time of rapid discovery in the field of physics, especially in Röntgen's special field of radiation. Radiation is the way energy moves. It's transmitted in the form of rays or waves or even particles. Röntgen, like other physicists, was curious to see the effects of different types of radiation. He had special equipment consisting of airtight tubes and cardboard shields (to block out light) so that he could bombard the tube with one type of radiation and then remove the cardboard and observe the effect.

During one of these tests, he noticed a strange colored shadow on the window. It could only have been caused by a light that had passed through the heavy cardboard shield. Röntgen knew of no kind of ray that could do that, so he called this mysterious radiation

"X-rays," following the scientific tradition of using the letter "X" to mean "unknown."

Röntgen continued to test this strange new ray, and it became clear that it could indeed pass through some objects (like flesh) but would leave a shadow to show where it was absorbed (for example, in bones). Just before Christmas,

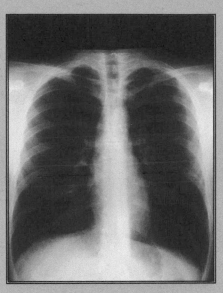

A modern-day chest X-Ray.

he called his wife, Anna, in to photograph her hand using X-rays. The result was a clear picture of her hand, with the bones (and her wedding ring) clearly visible. The overjoyed Röntgen could see how this would benefit science. His wife's reaction was a bit more down to earth, especially as she had just seen part of her own skeleton: "I have seen my death!"

Röntgen's discoveries in the field of radiation clearly paved the way for many scientific marvels, such as the X-ray machine, in the years to come—but it wasn't without its potentially catastrophic side, either. Obviously, any energy that can pass right through us can cause damage to our bodies—it all depends on the amount. While small doses of some kinds of radiation can help rid people of devastating illnesses like cancer by altering cells in our bodies, massive doses of radiation can actually kill us. Seems like Röntgen's wife got it kind of half right!

THE SCIENCE BEHIND IT

THE SCIENTIFIC WORLD WAS QUICK TO CELEBRATE Röntgen's discovery and to agree that he had made an enormous breakthrough (excuse the pun!) in helping doctors to study people's bones and other internal organs. Many scientists began calling them "Röntgen rays" in his honor, but their discoverer modestly insisted that they continue to be called X-rays.

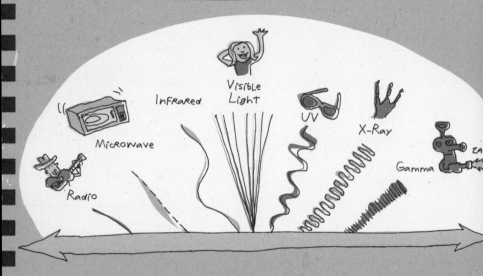

The Electromagnetic Spectrum

Just what are X-rays? Well, they are one of various types of radiation. Scientists classify these kinds of radiation by their wavelength, and they chart these different wavelengths (and the corresponding types of radiation) on a band called the electromagnetic spectrum. Visible light is one part of this spectrum. You have probably heard of some of the others, such as infrared light, ultraviolet light, radio waves, ultraviolet waves, and gamma rays. Scientists produce—or release—these different types of light by bombarding different materials with electrons. To produce X-rays, they bombard tungsten (a hard, metallic element) with electrons.

All of these different types share an important quality: They fan out in all directions, just as visible light does from the Sun or from an uncovered lightbulb. The difference comes from what stops them—and that is tied in with their wavelength again. If you hold your open hand in front of a flashlight, you can understand a bit more about this process.

X-rays work in a similar way, but they pass through the soft flesh as easily as visible light passes through glass or water. Bones, however, absorb X-rays. It is the shadows of the bones that we see so clearly when we look at an X-ray photograph, just as Anna Röntgen did in December 1895.

For many years, the only clear pictures we got from X-rays were of bones and hard substances. More recently, though, doctors have had patients swallow (or be injected with) liquids that absorb X-rays just as bones do. That means that we can now have accurate X-ray photographs of blood vessels and many "soft bits" inside our bodies.

EXPERIMENT 27

This experiment shows that it isn't just X-rays that can pass through the body, with some of them being absorbed along the way. Ordinary visible light can give you a version of the same result so that you can get an instant "X-ray vision" image of your hand. Of course, the result isn't quite as dramatic as a real X-ray image because a good deal of the visible light—unlike X-rays—gets absorbed by the body's soft tissue. Still, some of it does get through, giving you the spooky result.

MATERIALS

- A ROOM THAT CAN BE COMPLETELY DARKENED WITH CURTAINS, SHADES, ETC.

- POWERFUL FLASHLIGHT (BUT NARROWER THAN THE WIDTH OF YOUR PALM)

- FRIEND TO WITNESS THE SPOOKY RESULT

TAKE CARE!

Flashlights can get hot to the touch. Remove your hand if your flashlight starts feeling too warm—and turn your flashlight off to cool it down. Never point a flashlight into anyone's eyes.

1 Make sure the room is as dark as you can get it.

2 Turn the flashlight on and aim it at the center of a flat wall, and then turn it off.

3 Hold your palm against the flashlight, with your fingers tightly shut.

4 Turn the flashlight on and watch the images on the wall. You should be able to see faint shadows of the bones in your hand. You can move closer to the wall to get a clearer image of your bone shadows, but the "picture" will be smaller. If you're not seeing anything on the wall, then your flashlight needs to be stronger: Either check the batteries or try an even more powerful type of flashlight.

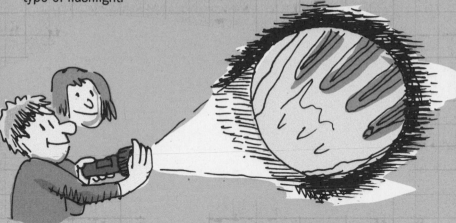

Röntgen's X-Ray Machine
EXPERIMENT 28

In this experiment you'll be making your own very simple X-ray machine. It will highlight another interesting feature of X-rays and other forms of radiation (including visible light): They behave like waves *and* like particles. The sand you'll be using represents the particle-like quality of X-rays. When you pour the sand over your X-ray machine, some of it will be absorbed by the pattern you've made while the rest passes through the screen just as X-rays pass through much of your body. When you take the screen and pattern away, you'll see an eerie "shadow" of the pattern on the base of the shoebox lid.

MATERIALS

- CARDBOARD SHOEBOX LID
- PIECE OF WINDOW SCREEN (LARGER THAN THE SHOEBOX LID)
- SCISSORS
- SHEET OF CONSTRUCTION PAPER
- PENCIL
- FINE SAND

TAKE CARE!

It's probably best to do this experiment outdoors so that you don't spill any sand on floors or carpets inside. Wait for a calm day or find a sheltered spot so that a breeze can't knock the pattern off the screen.

1 Lay the shoebox lid on the ground so that the rims point up.

2 Cut a piece of screen a bit bigger than the lid.

3 On the sheet of construction paper, trace a shape (a circle or star will work well). Make sure that the shape is smaller than the shoebox lid. Cut the shape out of the construction paper.

4 Put the screen on the shoebox lid so they both align, and then place the shape you cut out of construction paper on top of the screen, as close to the middle as you can get.

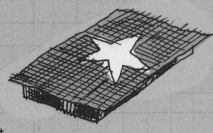

5 Sprinkle sand over the whole thing from directly above.

6 Remove the pattern and screen to reveal the "X-ray image" of the pattern.

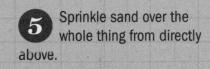

Marie Curie Discovers

RADIOACTIVE ISOTOPE

SO GOOD, THEY GAVE HER THE NOBEL PRIZE TWICE

A reptilian monster more than 400 feet tall pounds slowly toward Tokyo, sweeping aside buildings with every swing of its tail and scorching the Japanese countryside with its breath. Giant ants swarm over the mountains of New Mexico, sending locals running for cover. Wasps the size of school buses terrorize Central Africa while a California man gets smaller and smaller and smaller until he walks through the screen mesh of a cellar window.

Luckily, all of these stories are imaginary—the basic ideas behind the movies *Them!*, *Godzilla, Monster from Green Hell,* and

The Incredible Shrinking Man. Each of those films was made in the 1950s and each touched on the public's real fear of something mysterious, invisible, and deadly—radiation.

People in the 1950s could see the effects of radiation on the inhabitants of Hiroshima and Nagasaki, cities that were the targets of two atomic weapons in 1945 (see Fermi's Chain Reaction, page 217). While many inhabitants of the areas survived the initial blast, they continued to become ill and die for years afterward. Those illnesses and deaths were somehow linked to the aftereffects of the atomic explosions. But just what was radiation, and why was it so strong?

The search for the answers had actually begun more than 50 years earlier by Marie Curie, a Polish-born scientist working in France. Born in Warsaw in 1867, Maria Sklodowska went to study in Paris when she was 24. In 1894 she met the French physicist Pierre Curie and the pair were married the following year; Maria Sklodowska then became known as Marie Curie. Together with fellow scientist Henri Becquerel, the Curies began studying the chemical element uranium, which Becquerel had observed emitting radiation like X-rays (see page 163).

Marie found that the uranium ore actually emitted more radiation than the uranium itself. That led her to conclude that the radiation must be coming from other elements in the ore. These elements, like uranium, give off radiation as their nuclei (cores) break down. Marie Curie invented the term "radioactivity"

Marie Curie at work in her lab.

to describe this breaking down, and in 1898, she and her husband discovered two new radioactive elements —radium and polonium, which Marie named after her native country. Marie Curie, her husband, and Becquerel, were awarded the Nobel Prize in Physics for their work in radioactivity in 1903.

Radium was put to use as a cancer treatment (known as radiotherapy), and it became sought after because of its "glow in the dark" properties. In 1911, Marie Curie was awarded her second Nobel Prize (this time for chemistry) for isolating radium.

But the same radiation that helps control cancerous growths can also harm healthy parts of the body. If you've ever had an X-ray taken, you know that the technicians taking the X-ray will usually cover the part of your body not being X-rayed with a protective lead coat while they hightail it out of the room to "snap" your X-ray. That's because we now know that too much exposure to radiation can lead to something called "radiation sickness." Unfortunately, Marie Curie didn't know about this potentially catastrophic consequence of radiation back then, and didn't know to take the precautionary measures needed to protect herself from harmful rays. She constantly felt tired and was often depressed, symptoms, we now know, of radiation sickness, and in 1934 she died of a bone disease that is caused by prolonged exposure to radiation.

THE SCIENCE BEHIND IT

ONE OF THE GREAT THINGS ABOUT PHYSICS IS THAT it allows scientists to look at huge, massive objects such as stars and galaxies or at the tiniest of particles—the bits that make up atoms and sometimes the bits that make up those bits. But large or small, all of them tell us something about matter and energy.

Marie Curie's study of radiation took her on a route into the heart of matter, the building blocks of *everything*, and how they behave. It is important to realize that while she was coming up with her theory of atomic radioactivity, many scientists still doubted that atoms even existed (see "Einstein's Atom," page 191).

Everything that you can see around you—clouds, soda cans, sandals, teeth—is made up of a combination of atoms. And atoms themselves are made up of smaller (subatomic) particles called protons, neutrons, and electrons. Protons are positively-charged particles. They cluster together to form the center, or nucleus, of an atom. Electrons are negatively charged, and they circle around the nucleus like planets around the Sun. There are always the same number of protons as there are electrons, so they balance each other out.

Alpha, Beta, and Gamma: The three main types of radioactivity are named after the first three letters in the Greek alphabet. Alpha particles form when two protons and two neutrons are sent off from the atom. Beta particles form when one of the neutrons in the nucleus changes into a proton and an electron. The proton rejoins the nucleus but the new electron (the beta particle) is ejected at high speed. Each of these processes unleashes the release of high-energy gamma radiation.

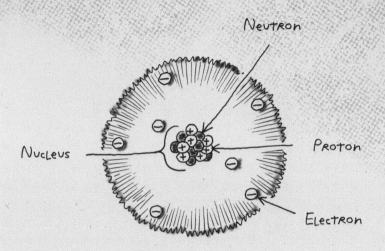

The number of protons in the nucleus of an atom is known scientifically as the atomic number—it's the unique "ID tag" of each chemical element. The simplest element, hydrogen, has only one proton and one electron. Gold, on the other hand, has 79 protons in its nucleus and 79 electrons orbiting around them.

There is also a third type of subatomic particle, the neutron. These guys have no charge (neutron—neutral . . . get it?), but they do have mass. Plus they use a powerful form of energy (called the "strong force" or even "nuclear glue") to bind the protons together in the nucleus. Remember that otherwise the positively charged protons would repel each other. The "heavier" elements—ones with the highest atomic numbers—are often unstable, with protons and neutrons bouncing around like crazy. Sometimes a particle will shoot right out of an atom in order to make it more stable, and when this happens, energy is released.

Radioactivity describes this process of energy release. Used carefully, it can help treat illnesses such as cancer. But prolonged exposure to radiation can lead to illness and death—as Marie Curie and the people of Hiroshima and Nagasaki found out.

Madame Curie's Popcorn Carbon Dating

EXPERIMENT 29

Archaeologists call on the principle of radioactive decay to help determine how old ancient objects are. They use a technique called carbon dating to work out the age of once-living things. Carbon dating measures the amount of a carbon isotope (called carbon 14) in something that has been found—an old bone, some leather, a tooth.

Radioactive materials such as carbon 14 break down at a predictable rate. All living things have a certain amount in them. Over time the amount of this type of carbon reduces as it "decays" into other forms. That predictable rate of decay is called a half-life. After 5,730 years, the object loses half of its carbon 14, and then another half goes in the next 5,730 years, and so on. By working out how much there is in an old object—and knowing that it started out with a certain amount—scientists can work out how long it took to reach that point.

You probably don't have thousands of years to spend on carbon dating but you can get an idea of how it works by figuring out the half-life of popcorn in this experiment. Like carbon 14, a kernel of corn on a hot pan is waiting to change to become more stable (by popping). Count up the number of kernels before you start and then try to see when half of them have popped. Then see how long it takes for half of *them* to pop, and so on. What you'll be doing is working out the half-life of the popcorn. But unlike archaeologists doing their carbon dating, you'll be able to eat your evidence.

MATERIALS

- POPCORN KERNELS
- PENCIL
- NOTE PAPER
- EMPTY DISH
- STOVE
- 1 TABLESPOON OF COOKING OIL
- FRYING PAN
- OVEN MITTS
- WATCH WITH SECOND HAND
- A FRIEND TO HELP TIME THE EXPERIMENT

TAKE CARE!

This experiment should be done under adult supervision, because hot oil can splatter.

1 Count out 16 popcorn kernels and set them aside.

2 Mark "8," "4," "2," and "1" on a piece of paper.

3 Set the empty dish on a counter near the stovetop.

4 Heat a tablespoon of oil in a frying pan.

5 Carefully add the 16 kernels to the pan and have your friend start timing.

6 Count the number of kernels that pop (probably right out of the pan) and tell your friend when eight have popped. She should mark the number of seconds by the "8" on the paper.

7 Continue to watch and tell your friend when four of the remaining eight have popped. She can mark this new time by the "4."

8 Then shout out when two of the remaining four have popped (that's the cue to mark the time by the "2").

9 Then call out when one of the last two has popped (and your friend logs the time by the "1").

10 You should see a similar amount of time passing between each stage: That time (enough for half of the remaining kernels to pop) is the "half-life" of the popcorn.

The Wright Brothers'
FLYING MACHINE

IT COULD BE A LONG WAY DOWN

Diary entry, December 17, 1903: "After running the engine and propellers a few minutes to get them in working order, I got on the machine at 10:35 for the first trial. . . . On slipping the rope, the machine started off increasing in speed to probably 7 or 8 miles (per hour). The machine lifted from the truck just as it was entering on the fourth rail. Mr. Daniels took a picture just as it left the tracks.

"I found the control of the front rudder quite difficult on account of its being balanced too near the center and thus had a tendency to turn itself when started so that the rudder was turned too far on one side and then too far on the other. As a result the machine would rise suddenly to about 10 feet and then as suddenly, on turning the rudder, dart for the ground. A sudden dart when out about 100 feet from the end of the tracks ended the flight. Time about 12 seconds (not known exactly as watch was not promptly stopped)."

Those words, so calm and matter-of-fact, were written by Orville Wright on the day he made history by making the first powered flight. Orville and his brother Wilbur had taken what had been a dream of Man for thousands of years—to fly like a bird—and turned it into a reality.

The Wright brothers were bike mechanics who had a workshop in Dayton, Ohio. In the 1890s even bicycles were seen as new and daring inventions, but the brothers wanted to take things further—and higher. They studied how birds flew and soared, and used these observations to build gliders large enough to hold an adult. By 1903, they were ready to test these gliders, and they chose Kitty Hawk, North Carolina, as their test site. There they made more than 700 glider flights.

They used their gliders as a model for the first plane, which they named the *Flyer*. By December, the *Flyer* was ready to live up to its name. Both brothers wanted to be the first to fly it, so they flipped a coin. Wilbur won, but his attempt on December 14 failed. It was Orville's turn next, and on December 17 he became the first person ever to fly a plane in the air. It lasted only 12 seconds, but it meant human beings had acquired the ability to fly. Later that same day, Wilbur took another stab at piloting the *Flyer*. This time he flew 800 feet and was in the air for 59 seconds.

The Wright brothers spent the rest of their lives honing what they learned about airplanes and making newer and better models. They also spent much of their time demonstrating the marvels of flight to amazed spectators on the ground, even taking passengers to fly with them. Then, five years after their first successful flight at Kitty Hawk, catastrophe struck. On September 17, 1908, Orville took Lieutenant Thomas E. Selfridge as a passenger on a flight in Fort Myers, Virginia. At 175 pounds, Selfridge was the heaviest passenger the Wrights had ever tried to transport. After three laps over the parade ground, the plane began to shake, and as Orville desperately tried to regain control to land, the plane began to nosedive at 75 feet off the ground. Orville sustained terrible injuries but lived. Selfridge was not so lucky, and went down in history as the first fatality in the history of aviation.

The first modern bikes, which were developed in Europe in the 1860s and called **bonecrushers** because of their wooden wheels, used pedals attached to the front wheel (like tricycles). In 1871, British engineer James Starley designed a bike with rubber tires. It was called the **penny-farthing** because its huge front wheel resembled a large British coin (penny) and its tiny rear wheel looked like the much smaller farthing coin. In 1885, Starley refined the design with inflatable tires and a chain linking the pedals to the rear wheel. Called the **safety bicycle** (because so many riders fell from the penny-farthing), it was the design that the Wright brothers used in their workshop.

THE WRIGHT BROTHERS WERE NOT THE FIRST people to believe it possible to build an aircraft that could take off and land using its own power. In fact, many people argue that they weren't even the first to make such a plane and fly it. Was it Melville M. Murrell of Tennessee in August 1877? Or maybe Richard Pearse of New Zealand on March 31, 1902? The Wright brothers are remembered because they made their plans clear, had witnesses, and continued to develop aircraft in later years. But Murrell, Pearse, and anyone else who might have been "first" would have had to use the same science and technology that the Wright brothers used.

Melville M. Murrell, an inventor from Hamblen County, Tennessee, invented an aircraft called the "American Flying Machine" in 1876. It was powered by the pilot, who operated cords and pulleys to cause the wings to flap up and down. Charlie Cowan, a hired hand on the Murrell farm, made several flights of more than 100 yards in August 1877.

Richard Pearse invented a motor-powered airplane (resembling a modern microlight aircraft) in 1902. He increased its engine power enough to make some test flights in March 1903, nine months before the Wright brothers' success at Kitty Hawk. Although in many ways Pearse's plane looked more modern than the Wright brothers' aircraft (it had one wing on each side and not two), he is largely forgotten because—unlike Orville and Wilbur—he never followed up his invention with improved designs.

What the Wright brothers, Murrell, and Pearse all had in common was the key to flight, which is aerodynamics. For something to become airborne, it must perform a balancing act with four forces: lift, weight, thrust, and drag. Lift is what a plane needs to rise up off the ground. The shape of the wings is what gives an airplane enough lift to overcome its weight. By

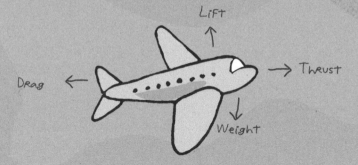

weight we mean gravity, the force that keeps everything on this planet from simply floating away. An airplane has to fight gravity to take off, and it does this with the help of thrust. Nowadays an airplane achieves thrust, which is forward motion, with propellers or a jet engine, but early aircraft used nothing more than the pedalling of a bike to achieve forward motion (it was not a coincidence that the Wright brothers were bicycle makers!). Once it's in the air, an airplane continues to need thrust or it will stall in midair, lose all its lift, and fall. The fourth force vital to an airplane flying is drag, which is air resistance. This is the force that slows a plane down. It's the combination of all four of these forces acting in equilibrium that maintains an airplane's steady flight. Lift must balance weight and thrust must balance drag when the plane flies at constant velocity. It's when one force overcomes the other that the airplane comes down.

> The word **aerodynamic** is derived from a combination of two Greek words—**aeros**, meaning "air," and **dynamis**, meaning "power."

Orville's Aerodynamics
EXPERIMENT 30

This experiment is all about the first force of aerodynamics: lift. It will show you how lift works with an airplane wing in a combination of motion and pressure. In this case, the faster the air moves, the less pressure (force) it exerts. That is the basis of Bernoulli's Principle, named for the Swiss scientist who first noted it in the 18th century. An airplane wing is based on a shape known as an airfoil: The top is slightly curved and the bottom is straight. As a plane moves, the air traveling across the curved top must go faster than the air below in order to meet up at the other end. And as it picks up speed, it loses pressure, so that the pressure from below becomes stronger and stronger until . . . takeoff.

MATERIALS

- NEWSPAPER
- SCISSORS
- HARDBOUND BOOK
- ELECTRIC FAN
- BUBBLE GUM

TAKE CARE!
Never let your fingers get too close to a fan!

1 Cut a piece of newspaper to about 12 inches by 3 inches.

2 Slide the paper into the book as though it were a bookmark, with about half sticking out.

3 Hold the book with the paper at the top and swing your arm through the air. The paper should rise up because of Bernoulli's Principle.

4 Take the paper from the book and hold one of its short sides about 12 inches in front of an electric fan. Again, the air blowing across it should make the top rise up.

5 Dab a tiny piece of your bubble gum (the one you've been chewing!) to the end of the paper and hold it up again to the fan. See how many more pieces of gum you need to add before it stops working.

Wilbur's Flying Machine

EXPERIMENT (31)

The second experiment lets you try out some of the other forces at work in flight. Remember, once a plane is airborne, there is still the matter of steering it. Pilots do this by raising and lowering flaps on the wings and tail of the plane. A full-size plane has flaps that can be made to go up and down on each wing, as well as on the tail. The flaps on the wings are called ailerons and are used to steer the plane left or right. Those on the tail are called elevators, which should give you a clue as to their role—helping the plane go up or down. Your plane, of course, has only one wing on each side, so the flaps you make will work as both ailerons and elevators—but not at the same time.

MATERIALS

- **4 PIECES OF 8½-INCH X 11-INCH PAPER**
- **SCISSORS**
- **THREE FRIENDS**

TAKE CARE!

Paper planes have never posed much of a health or danger risk. Make sure, though, that you have some spare pieces of paper in case you have a crash—or if some friends show up and want to make their own.

1 Your three friends and you are going to be folding paper airplanes—each one demonstrating a different aeronautic principle. To start out, all of you should fold the same exact type of paper airplane. First, fold your sheet of paper in half lengthwise, and then fold and flatten down a triangle out from the center about 3 inches from the end.

2 Repeat again, this time folding the new triangle over the first just more than halfway down the length of the paper.

3 Finish with one more fold, this time making the crease about halfway along each short side.

4 Give your planes a few test flights.

5 Now you're all going to customize your planes. You go first. Cut a line about an inch back from the end of your plane on each side so that the tail-end wings have flaps. Fold both flaps UP.

6 Have friend #1 cut a line about an inch back from the end of his/her plane on each side so that the tail-end wings have flaps. Fold both flaps DOWN.

7 Have friend #2 cut a line about an inch back from the end of his/her plane on each side so that the tail-end wings have flaps. Fold the left flap UP and the right one DOWN.

8 Then have friend #3 cut a line about an inch back from the end of the plane on each side so that the tail-end wings have flaps. Fold the right flap UP and the left one DOWN.

9 All of you stand in a line and, at the count of three, launch your planes into the air. This is what *should* happen: Friend #1's plane will rise up because the flaps are playing the role of elevators, making the air hitting against it literally tilt the plane upward. Friend #2's plane will go down because the elevators, pointing down, stop the flow of air underneath, causing the plane to head downward. Friend #3's plane will veer to the right and friend #4's plane will veer to the left because the flaps are now acting as ailerons.

Einstein's ATOM

ALBERT HEARS A WHO

How can you prove something exists if it's invisible? If you remember your Dr. Seuss, then you may remember the story of good old Horton, an elephant with a similar dilemma. Horton had found a tiny speck of dust on which he knew:

". . . there were people of very small size, Too small to be seen by an elephant's eyes."

No one in the jungle believed Horton, but luckily for all those tiny people on that tiny dust speck, they were able to raise enough of a ruckus to finally prove to the world that they *did* exist. And lucky for us—Einstein did the same thing in 1905 when he published his paper "A New Measurement of Molecular Dimensions & on the Motion of Small Particles Suspended in a Stationary Liquid."

Up until then, most people didn't quite understand that matter—everything we are, everything we see and touch—is made up of molecules so small they can't be seen with the naked eye. But the scientifically curious had come to that conclusion, even if they couldn't work out why. About 2,500 years ago, Greek scientists figured that all living and nonliving things must be made up of invisible and indivisible particles. They called these theoretical particles atoms, from the Greek word *atomos* ("undivided"). Hindu philosophers in India, pondering about the nature of matter, came to a similar conclusion.

It took more than 2,300 years for those Greek and Indian ideas to give birth to a coherent theory about the ultimate makeup of matter—that atoms really do lie at the heart of this universe. But suddenly, in the 20th century, some scientists began to believe that atoms couldn't possibly exist because new scientific theories about heat had no room for them.

Einstein restored the notion of atoms and molecules existing in the real world because he married the new theories about heat

Molecular theory: Scientists are on a constant quest to find the most basic building blocks of all matter. We know that molecules are made up of atoms and that atoms are made up of electrons, protons, and neutrons. Protons and neutrons, in turn, are made up of quarks. This branch of science is called high-energy physics, because some of the tiniest subatomic (smaller than an atom) particles are created only when other particles collide at incredibly high speeds.

Hiroshima: The world saw the power of atomic energy in action for the first time on August 6, 1945, when the United States dropped an atomic bomb on the Japanese city of Hiroshima. The bomb exploded with the force of 13,000 tons of the explosive TNT, creating a circle of total destruction two miles across. Up to 140,000 people died because of the blast, many of them suffering burns from the radiation.

with Newton's tried and trusted Laws of Motion (see page 83). This contribution provided substance to the theory of tiny atoms combining to form molecules, and those molecules in turn sticking together to form insects, trees, humans, and even planets and stars. You can picture this by imagining one atom as being a Lego. Stick several together, and you have a molecule. Then combine a lot of those stuck-together Legos, and you get a toy (or an organism, if you're using molecules).

Scientists would go on to reveal that despite what the Greeks had stated, atoms can be divided, or "split." And when they are, they release enormous amounts of energy. Sometimes that energy release can be controlled (see Fermi, page 217). At other times it can be channeled into devastating weapons . . . or a potentially catastrophic release of atomic energy.

THE SCIENCE BEHIND IT

ATOMIC THEORY REMAINED JUST THAT, A THEORY— or worse yet, ignored and forgotten for many centuries after the Greeks and Indians first developed it. About 900 years ago, Arab scientists dusted it down in an effort to show how everything—including the movement of the tiniest particles—depended on God's will.

Once Europe embarked on its Scientific Revolution, a continent-wide burst of observation and theorizing beginning in the 16th century, atoms came back to center stage. Some scientists figured that the Greeks were on to a good thing, but had no way of working out whether they were right or wrong. In the 19th century, though, things moved forward pretty quickly. The English chemist John Dalton (1766–1844) was working with chemical elements such as carbon and oxygen and saw that they combined in certain multiples of their respective weights. Dalton's work led to his atomic theory in 1803—he proposed that each atom of a particular element had an identical mass that was different from the mass of any other element's atoms.

Then in 1827, a Scottish botanist named Robert Brown (1773–1858) noticed that pollen grains placed into a clear liquid behaved strangely, moving around randomly as if they were alive though there was no visible impetus to make them move. This mysterious effect became known as Brownian Motion.

Brownian Motion was actually the key to Einstein's 1905 breakthrough: He stated that in fact the

We owe much of what we know about
the universe to Albert Einstein.

pollen was being moved around by the molecules
(and their component parts, atoms). What Einstein
did was come up with a way of measuring those
molecules. That meant he was able to predict their
randomness precisely—even to the point of deter-
mining the dimensions of hypothetical molecules.

Einstein's ability to apply statistical methods to
the random motions of atoms using mathematical
formulas, confirmed where possible by experimental observation, led to his groundbreaking *General
Theory of Relativity,* published in 1916. Using that
theory, Einstein and other scientists were able to
understand how the universe works. The Big Bang,
black holes, dark matter: All of these scientific and
conceptual breakthroughs came about as a result of
Albert Einstein's extraordinary mind.

Einstein's Magical Atom

EXPERIMENT 32

This experiment almost seems to be a magic trick—surely adding one cup of rubbing alcohol to one cup of water gives us two cups of that combined liquid? Actually, the answer is no, because some of the alcohol molecules find their way into spaces between the water molecules. It's a bit like adding a cup of water to a cup of marbles.

MATERIALS

- WATER
- MEASURING CUP
- 2-PINT CLEAR GLASS CONTAINER (WITH FRACTIONS OF CUPS MARKED ON IT)
- ISOPROPYL (RUBBING) ALCOHOL
- GOGGLES

TAKE CARE!

Don't let any small children near the rubbing alcohol, and make sure you wear the goggles to protect your eyes from splashes when you pour in the alcohol.

1 Carefully measure 1 cup of water and pour it into the 2-pint container. (Your measurements must be exact for the experiment to work.)

2 Carefully measure 1 cup of rubbing alcohol and add it to the water. Again, be exact!

3 Now take a precise reading of the amount of liquid in the container. It should come to less than 2 cups (1 pint).

Einstein's Brownian Motion
EXPERIMENT 33

This experiment shows that molecules are moving around even if we can't see them. A few drops of food coloring will simply remain little blobs of strong color in clear water unless you stir them in, right? Well, the water molecules themselves will probably do all that stirring themselves if you give them time—just remember that Brownian Motion.

MATERIALS

- WATER
- GLASS JAR (ABOUT 12-16 FLUID OUNCES)
- FOOD COLORING

TAKE CARE!

Make sure you choose a dark food coloring because it highlights the dramatic payoff better.

1 Fill the jar about halfway with water.

2 Add several drops of food coloring. They should be clearly visible as a darker color even as they sink to the bottom.

3 Leave the jar still for three hours.

4 Observe the liquid again—it should be all one color, as if the food coloring had been stirred in.

Robert Goddard's
ROCKET SHIP

MAYBE IT *IS* ROCKET SCIENCE, AFTER ALL

Professor Robert Goddard of Clark University in Massachusetts was a quiet man who went about his studies without attracting much publicity. That is, until 1919, when he published a paper on his special subject—rockets and rocket science. In it, he described experiments with different fuels that could send rockets into the sky at great speed. He also touched on the subject of sending the rocket out of the Earth's atmosphere—even as far as the Moon!

Somehow *The New York Times* learned of the paper and published a mocking

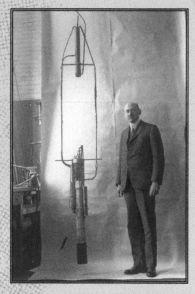
Robert Goddard in his laboratory.

criticism of Goddard, saying that his idea of traveling to the Moon showed that he lacked "the knowledge ladled out daily in high schools."

Goddard probably had that criticism still ringing in his ears on March 16, 1926, when he set up a 10-foot rocket (called "Nell") in a field on his Aunt Effie's farm. The rocket looked frail and weak as it stood on its stand. But inside was something that no rocket had ever used before: liquid fuel. Goddard had developed a mixture of gasoline and liquid oxygen—the type of mixture that he said could eventually work in a rocket to the Moon.

An assistant lit the fuse with a blowtorch attached to a pole, and the rocket shot upward, reaching a height of only 41 feet before crashing into the ground 180 feet away. The flight might have been short—but so was Orville Wright's (see page 181). And with it, the Space Age had begun.

We might look back at Goddard's achievement and think "space shuttles," "satellites," and even "Man on the Moon." After all, NASA's main research center is called the Goddard Space Flight Center. But few people at the time realized Goddard's achievement.

Still, there was one scientist about 4,000 miles away who was very interested—and that's where the potentially catastrophic comes into play. That scientist's name was Wernher von Braun, who in the coming years would become one of the leading scientists working for Adolf Hitler's Nazi government. Von Braun said he was inspired by Goddard's methods to develop a powerful rocket, the V-2, which the German armed forces used during World War II. The V-2, which stood for "vengeance weapon 2," was a 12-ton rocket with a thrust of 250,000 newtons, a one-ton payload, and a range of about 200 miles. In the last months of the war, Germany launched more than 3,000 of these rockets, 1,300 of them on London alone. In what became known as "the Blitz," the Germans bombed London for 57 consecutive nights, killing more than 43,000 civilians and destroying over a million homes. Since the V-2s flew higher and faster than airplanes, Britain had no way of intercepting them, and the attack was curtailed only after the German army was driven back beyond the rocket's range.

Goddard went on to develop better and faster liquid-fuel rockets but didn't live to see them used in what had been his primary dream: to reach the Moon. On July 17, 1969, the day after *Apollo 11* set off for the first Moon landing mission, *The New York Times* printed the following apology for its scathing article almost 50 years earlier:

"Further investigation and experimentation have confirmed the findings of Isaac Newton in the 17th century and it is now definitely established that a rocket can function in a vacuum as well as in an atmosphere. The *Times* regrets the error."

Goddard would have been pleased.

THE SCIENCE BEHIND IT

ANY SORT OF ROCKET—A FIREWORK, A SPACE rocket, or even a balloon that has been let loose— demonstrates the same basic scientific principles. One of the most important is known as Newton's Third Law of Motion, which states that for every action there is an opposite and equal reaction. So when you take an inflated balloon and untie it, the air comes rushing out. Isaac Newton would identify that rushing air as the action. And the *re*-action is the way the balloon goes flying off.

The explosion of gunpowder, with its sudden burst of rushing exhaust, is a similar example of Newton's Third Law. The Chinese, as we know, used gunpowder to launch "fireworks" that, for all intents and purposes, worked very much like Goddard's rockets. But what Goddard realized was that gunpowder had its limits when it came to packing a real punch for a rocket. To power large rockets—and then send them across long distances—you need a far more powerful explosive. That is where the liquid fuel came into play in Goddard's "Nell."

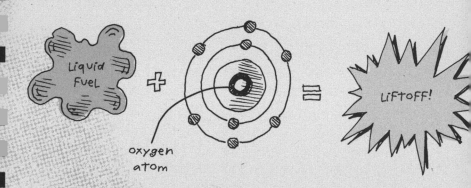

Liquid Fuel + oxygen atom = LiftOff!

Robert Goddard teaching physics at Clark University in 1914.

By using liquid oxygen as a component—along with gasoline—in the fuel that powered the rocket, Goddard solved the tricky problem of propelling a rocket after its initial launch off the ground. Goddard, who was already looking ahead to space travel, knew that explosives wouldn't combust (burn) in the airless surroundings of outer space because combustion needs oxygen (see page 57).

And that, of course, was the key to the future of rocket science, the germ of knowledge that would power the rocket that sent astronauts to the Moon and space probes to the outer edge of our solar system and beyond. And in one of the strangest twists of history, who should be the scientist who helped guide the United States space program into outer space and then to the Moon? A certain Wernher von Braun, who moved to the U.S. after World War II ended.

Robert Goddard's
Soda Bottle Rocket
EXPERIMENT 34

This experiment gives you a chance to build a rocket with liquid fuel—well, sort of. And it is as good a test of Newton's Third Law as any space flight.

MATERIALS

- EMPTY 2-LITER SODA BOTTLE
- SCISSORS
- STIFF CARDBOARD
- SCOTCH TAPE
- HAMMER
- NAIL
- CORK STOPPER (LIKE THE KIND IN A WINE BOTTLE) TO FIT SNUGLY INTO THE SODA BOTTLE MOUTH
- ADAPTER PIN FOR INFLATING BASKETBALLS OR FOOTBALLS

- 8 FEET OF PLASTIC TUBING (FROM HARDWARE STORE): TAKE BIKE PUMP TO STORE AND CHOOSE TUBING THAT FITS EASILY INTO THE PUMP
- WATER
- BIKE FLOOR PUMP (UPRIGHT)

TAKE CARE!
The rocket can go off at an angle, so you *must* have a car or wall as a barrier between you and the rocket.

1 The "rocket" will be the empty bottle, turned upside down, so the first step will be to add cardboard fins to raise the mouth of the bottle about 3 inches off the ground.

2 Cut 3 pieces of cardboard to make the fins. They should have a flat edge that can be taped onto the side of the bottle and a flat (not pointed) base so the bottle can rest on them.

3 Tape the fins on and test the bottle to see whether it will stand upright. Make alterations if necessary.

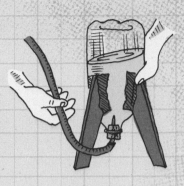

4 Hammer the nail through the center of the cork to make a hole. Then slide the adapter pin through the hole so it comes all the way through to the other side of the cork. The adapter pin should fit snugly inside.

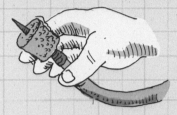

5 Connect the end of the adapter with one end of the plastic tubing. This will give you a distance of 8 feet between you and the rocket during liftoff. YOU MUST STAND BEHIND A PROTECTIVE BARRIER, SUCH AS A WALL OR A PARKED CAR, POSITIONED BETWEEN YOU AND THE ROCKET.

6 Fill the bottle $\frac{1}{3}$ full of water and then fit the cork in snugly; the other end is in place at the pump.

7 Turn the rocket over very gently so that it stands upright.

8 Make sure everyone is as far away from the liftoff site as possible. MAKE SURE WHOEVER IS PUMPING THE BICYCLE PUMP IS BEHIND THE PROTECTIVE BARRIER.

9 Pump steadily: The pressure builds up inside the bottle until it blows the stopper off and launches.

Igor Sikorsky's HELICOPTER

THE ONLY WAY IS UP

It was only after the Wright brothers' triumph in 1903—paving the way for powered flight—that engineers seriously considered making a helicopter. The idea had been around for centuries. In the mid-1500s, Leonardo da Vinci made drawings of what he called an ornithopter, a flying machine that looked suspiciously like a modern-day helicopter. And in 1784, the French inventor Christian de Launoy created a rotary-winged toy that could take off from the ground and fly. It was another Frenchman, a writer named Ponton d'Amécourt, who coined the term "helicopter" in 1863. (In Greek *helico* means "spiral," and *pter* means "winged.") And yet another Frenchman, Paul Cornu, is credited with having designed and flown the first real rotary-wing craft, which was similar to—but not the same as—a helicopter. The serious exploration of building a helicopter to actually transport a human being into the air was not taken seriously until after the Wright brothers took off at Kitty Hawk. Why? Well, because while the advantages were obvious, the potential for risk seemed catastrophic: Airplanes were scary enough, but at least they had wings to help a stalled plane glide down to the ground. With a helicopter there are NO wings—now that could be a *long* way down!

For the first 30 years of the 20th century, aircraft engineers in France, Spain, Argentina, and Russia raced to produce the first working helicopter—a craft that could not only take off and land safely but travel for long distances without landing. Some of their earliest attempts, like Cornu's, would fly for only a few seconds before crashing down to the ground—hard. They were also impossible to steer.

It was the Germans who came up with the first truly successful helicopter, the FA-61, in 1936. In one series of flights on June 25 and 26, pilot Ewald Rohlfs set helicopter records for altitude (8,000 feet), length of flight (1 hour, 20 minutes), and distance in a straight line (50 miles). But the FA-61 was little more than an open-cockpit plane whose wings had been replaced with two upward-pointing propellers. The fuselage (central tube) still looked like a plane's, and so did its tail. Which is why the father of helicopters is not thought to be the German behind the invention of the FA-61, but a Russian-born inventor named Igor Sikorsky (1889–1972).

Sikorsky had begun working on helicopters in 1910, but it wasn't until 1940 that his VS-300 helicopter (Vought-Sikorsky 300) became the model for the modern helicopter. This was the first helicopter that could safely and predictably fly forward, backward, up, down, and sideways.

Of course—as has been proven again and again—it was the military application of most great inventions that made them potentially catastrophic. The helicopter was no exception, and Sikorsky followed up his VS-300 with the XR-4, the United States Army's first military helicopter.

While helicopters were used in World War II, it was in the Korean War that they began to reach their full potential—scouting out the terrain, delivering supplies and water to units in areas where planes couldn't land, getting in and out of combat areas quickly to transport wounded soldiers to safety.

It was the Vietnam War, though, that was the first real helicopter war. By the mid-1960s, the U.S. Army began moving masive amounts of troops by air into the jungles of Vietnam. Helicopters were equipped with guns and rockets that could rain terror on enemy combatants below from a relatively close distance.

A U.S. Army helicopter in Vietnam.

THE SCIENCE BEHIND IT

JUST ABOUT EVERYONE HAS THROWN PAPER PLANES or those lightweight balsa-wood gliders. It's pretty easy to see that an aircraft, even with no power, can glide in for a soft landing. Who can forget the sight of that passenger jet, with failed engines, coming down lower and lower past skyscrapers and then gliding to a safe landing on the Hudson River in New York City in 2009? Even the space shuttle glides back to Earth after its missions in outer space.

The one thing that links all of these aircraft is wings. It seems only natural that when human beings tried to make flying machines, they would begin their designs by looking at creatures that flew naturally— birds, bats, butterflies, and other winged creatures. But what if you want to take off and land in a tight space, like in the middle of a city or in a small clearing in the forests of Oregon? There's no room for a runway, so that rules airplanes out. And that's where helicopters come into the picture.

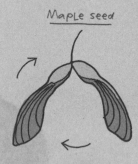

Maple seed

Just as nature provided us with inspiration for the first airplanes, it also provided some inspiration for helicopters. Just think of those maple seed "propellers" floating down from maple trees every spring. Chinese children played with their own versions of spinning-propeller toys 2,500 years ago, and Leonardo da Vinci was also probably inspired by those same "floating" seedlings when he designed his ornithopter.

The key to helicopter design is the rotor blade, the big propeller that provides the lift (upward force). It can be combined with smaller propellers to make the flight more stable, but that main propeller is the driving force. Like an airplane wing, it has an airfoil shape (see page 186) to increase the force it produces, and each blade is slightly angled. Think of this angle as an extra way of helping the blade or propeller "screw" through the air: In fact, the British still sometimes refer to propellers as airscrews. Helicopter rotor blades need to be big because they are also doing the job of an airplane's lift-producing wings.

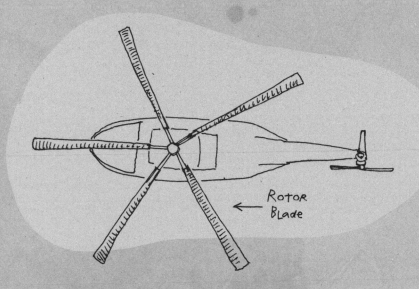

Rotor Blade

Sikorsky's Helicopter
EXPERIMENT 35

This experiment is a simple way to see helicopter propellers in action. In a way it is an echo of those maple-seed propellers, showing how helicopters can use the same principles of displacing air to float down to earth slowly.

MATERIALS

- SCISSORS
- PAPER
- RULER
- PENCIL

> **TAKE CARE!**
> It can take a bit of practice to get the folds just right. Remember that the most important thing is to have flaps A and B going out in opposite directions. Seen side-on, the helicopter looks like a capital T.

1 Cut a piece of paper into a rectangle 11 inches long by 2 inches wide. You can refer to the picture here to see how to mark out and cut the flaps of your paper propeller.

2 Use a ruler and pencil to mark out the paper as you see it in the illustration here. (Make sure you label each flap with its letter.)

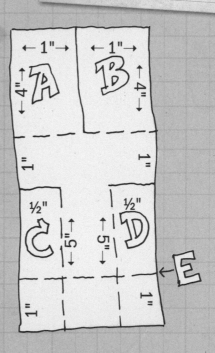

3 Carefully cut along every solid line and fold along the dotted lines.

4 Along the dotted line, fold flap A forward and flap B to the back.

5 Fold flaps C and D forward along the dotted lines so they meet.

6 Now fold line E up (which helps to lock C and D together).

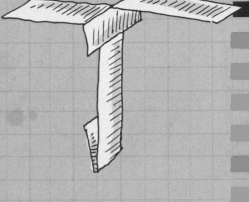

7 The helicopter should be ready to fly if you hold it by pinching flaps C and D and having A and B jutting in opposite directions to each other but parallel to the floor.

8 Hold the helicopter as high as you can and then let go and pull your hand away as fast as you can. The helicopter should swirl slowly down to the ground.

EXPERIMENT 36

This experiment is a way of saying something like "What comes down must go up." It shows how the same curve and angle that help a helicopter blade act like a brake actually drive the helicopter upward by giving it lift. With some careful bending and folding, you should be able to perfect an effective airfoil design.

TAKE CARE!

You'll probably need to adjust the curve of the blade and the amount that the flaps are folded. Be patient and you should achieve liftoff.

MATERIALS

- STIFF CARDBOARD
- RULER
- SCISSORS
- SHARP WOODEN PENCIL (OCTAGONAL, NOT ROUND)
- GLUE

1 Measure and cut out an 8-inch by 1-inch strip of cardboard.

2 Use the pencil or scissors to poke a small hole in the exact center of this strip.

3 Snip off a triangle from two diagonally opposite corners (for example, top right and bottom left) half an inch in from each side.

4 Measure 3 inches in from one non-snipped corner and make a mark on the edge of the cardboard wing, and then make another mark half an inch farther toward the center.

5 Cut half an inch in from the first (3-inch) mark, cutting perpendicularly to the wing.

6 Cut from the second (3½-inch) mark diagonally across to meet the end of the previous cut and remove the right triangle of cardboard.

7 Repeat steps 4, 5, and 6 along the other non-snipped wing edge.

8 Gently hold both long edges of the blade and curve the blade slightly; fold the 3-inch flaps downward a bit further than the curve of the blade.

9 Carefully push the pencil, point first, about an inch through the hole in the center of the cardboard. Make sure it is level and use a little glue to secure it against the pencil. Don't use too much glue, and make sure to let it dry before proceeding to step 10.

10 Hold the pencil below the wing between the palms of your hands.

11 Slowly slide one hand forward and the other hand back, and then do the opposite much more quickly and let go.

12 Your helicopter should take off and fly upward before losing speed and drifting down again.

Fermi's
CHAIN REACTION

BUT CAN HE STOP IT?

E nrico Fermi (1901–1954) was an Italian physicist whose study of neutrons, the tiny particles (with no electrical charge) that are inside atoms, won him the Nobel Prize in Physics in 1938. After collecting the prize in Sweden, though, Fermi and his wife, Laura, moved to the United States, where Fermi got a job at Columbia University alongside the Danish scientist Niels Bohr.

Fermi and Bohr knew that atoms—the tiny building blocks of all matter—were held together with huge amounts of energy. But research in the early 20th century

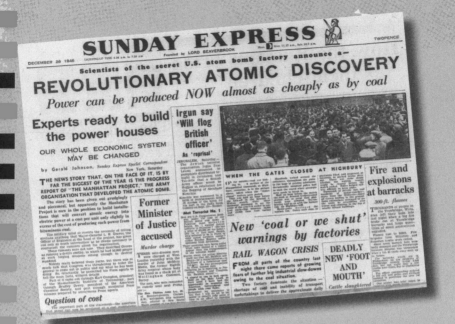

suggested that it was possible to split atoms apart, releasing that energy. Would that released energy be enough to split more atoms? The two scientists concentrated on the idea of an atomic "chain reaction," a series of atom splittings where the power of one split atom would be enough to split another, then another, and so on—like a row of dominoes being knocked down. Such a chain reaction could unleash enormous amounts of energy, which could be used to make incredibly powerful bombs. Fermi, Bohr, and other leading scientists such as Hungarian Leo Szilard realized this; they also knew that Adolf Hitler's scientists would be trying to create such an "atomic bomb." Szilard wrote a letter warning President Franklin D. Roosevelt of what would happen if Nazi Germany did develop "the Bomb" first.

Albert Einstein, at that time the most famous scientist in the world (and by then living in the United States), agreed about the terrible consequences of Germany's developing atomic weapons. Although years later he would regret helping to develop atomic weapons, he delivered the letter to the president on October 11, 1939. World War II had begun just a month earlier, and President Roosevelt hoped that Americans would eventually join in the fight against Hitler's Nazi regime. In the meantime, he approved a secret plan for the United States to study atomic power more closely. Three years later, this secret study would develop into an all-out effort to produce atomic weapons—the Manhattan Project.

The Manhattan Project was begun when the U.S. government decided to go full-out to produce an atomic weapon in August 1942. Although this effort would eventually cost $2 billion and employ more than 130,000 people, it was shrouded in secrecy and known only by its codename, the Manhattan Engineer District, or simply the Manhattan Project. Its scientific director was the physicist J. Robert Oppenheimer. The two atomic bombs dropped on Japan in August 1945 were the result of the Manhattan Project efforts.

The first step was to produce a controlled chain reaction. That word **controlled** is important. What would happen if the chain reaction couldn't be stopped? It was bad enough thinking of the Nazis with atomic bombs, but what about uncontrollable releases of energy? It could mean the end of the world!

Fermi found what he believed was a way of controlling the chain reaction (see "The Science Behind It"). So, on December 2, 1942, he set up his test lab in a squash court at the University of Chicago. Fermi and his assistants began the experiment . . . and then waited. The chain reaction did begin, but more important, the team was able to speed it up, slow it down, and then stop it. When the experiment was successfully completed, a message (in secret code) was sent to President Franklin D. Roosevelt: "The Italian navigator has landed in the new world."

Fermi's note suggested that the chain-reaction experiment went according to plan and that it was almost a formality going through the motions of what he had already decided in theory. But the truth remained that the behavior of subatomic particles at that time was full of uncertainty, and the consequences of an uncontrolled chain reaction—a growing series of energy releases spreading possibly across the entire planet—were in Fermi's mind from the start to the finish.

THE SCIENCE BEHIND IT

THE EARLY 20TH CENTURY SAW GREAT ADVANCES in how scientists understood atoms, the "building blocks" of matter. In particular, it became clear that huge amounts of energy were locked inside atoms. If those atoms could be pulled apart—or "split"—then that energy could be released.

The term *radioactivity* describes the release of energy from atoms that decay, or come apart. This happened naturally, but over long periods of time. What Fermi and other scientists were looking for was a way of releasing that energy far more quickly. And the way to do that would be to split atoms and then use some of the energy that was released to split more. And these in turn would split more, to create the chain reaction.

Fermi had first noted that getting an atom to absorb an extra neutron would cause it to split. You couldn't really call that the easy bit, but even so, there's a tougher bit to come up with: How could Fermi *control* this chain reaction if he didn't want the whole city of Chicago—and maybe the world—to be destroyed by all that energy? His solution was to find rods that would absorb neutrons, slowing or even stopping the chain reaction.

The result meant that scientists had a choice. They could generate a steady flow of energy by controlling the chain reaction—in the way nuclear power stations do. Or they could allow an uncontrolled chain reaction to go on producing vast amounts of energy as all the atoms in a supply of fuel were used up

A nucLeaR chain Reaction:

A neutRon collides with a uRanium atom, causing it to split into 2 smaLLeR atoms and ReLease eneRgy as well as a neutRon. This neutRon then collides with anotheR uRanium atom . . . and so on and so FoRth.

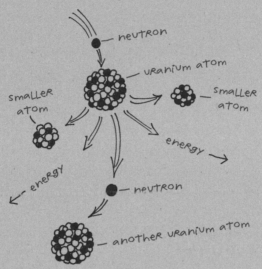

quickly. That second method was—and is—the basis of atomic bombs. It is guessed that a single 500-kiloton nuclear bomb would instantly incinerate 60,000 people—with another one and a half million people dying within a week from the effects of the radiation, and another five million or so dying in the months following. And if children are warned about playing with fire, who was there to remind the scientists about the catastrophic results of playing with atoms?

J. Robert Oppenheimer was the dedicated and patriotic scientific director of the Manhattan Project, guiding the research and tests at every stage. But he never lost sight of the devastating potential of atomic weapons. When the first atomic bomb was tested in New Mexico on July 16, 1945, Oppenheimer recalled a line from Hindu scripture: "I am become Death, the destroyer of worlds."

Fermi's Chain Reaction
EXPERIMENT 37

This experiment doesn't involve radioactivity, but it is a good way to get you to think about chain reactions. It is also one of the easiest, hardest, strangest, funniest, quickest, most time-consuming experiments in the whole book—depending on your point of view and what you make of it. But before you read ahead, remember that whatever you do is meant to help you understand the idea of a chain reaction. And a chain reaction is pretty much just what it says. It involves a series of steps or stages that are connected in some way.

For example, you could set up a chain reaction that begins with letting a marble go down a ramp set up on an ironing board until it rolls into a plastic cup on the edge, which gets knocked off the ironing board but is tied to the board with a string so it swings into a row of dominoes, and then the last domino falls and . . . well, you get the picture.

It all boils down to using your own imagination—and as many things as the nearest grown-ups will let you borrow. Just remember that you can't use any plug-in electrical item (battery-operated toys are OK, though) and you shouldn't set the experiment up so that anything valuable could break.

MATERIALS

Below are some of the ingredients that people have used to do this experiment. You don't have to use any of them, but they are all useful:

- MARBLES
- RAMP OR TUNNEL FOR MARBLES OR TOY CARS
- IRONING BOARD WITH COVER OFF (YOU CAN FEED STRINGS THROUGH THE HOLES)
- PING-PONG BALLS
- FUNNEL
- RULER AND PENCIL (TO MAKE A SEESAW)
- STRING
- BUBBLE GUM
- EMPTY CD CASE

TAKE CARE!

You can use water (being filled up in one of the stages), but if you do, make sure you're doing the experiment either outside or in a garage so that you don't get things soaked in the house.

CATASTROPHE METER : **SLIGHT RISK OF MESS**

1 You will be constructing a chain reaction using as many different ingredients as you can find—or get to work together.

2 Set up the ironing board (with its cover off) and tie two pieces of string to it so that they hang down almost to the floor.

3 Stick a marble to each lower end of string with a bit of bubble gum.

4 Pull back on one string and let it swing toward the other. Untie the upper knot to raise or lower the string so that you get a direct hit.

5 When you've got that pair working, make a note of where and how far the second marble (the one that gets hit) swings. Stand the empty CD case there.

6 Now repeat step 4 so that you have the making of a chain reaction: Marble 1 hits marble 2, which knocks CD case over. (Replace the ingredients in their original position.)

7 Set up a seesaw made from a ruler balanced on a pencil so that the side hanging in the air will be hit by the CD case when it is knocked over. Repeat step 4 once again—now you have a new stage in the chain reaction.

8 Try to think of what you could put on the other side of the seesaw so that next time you'll have it sent into the air when marble 1 hits marble 2, which knocks the CD case over, which triggers the seesaw.

9 Continue adding stages to create an even bigger chain reaction, always noting where each element was.

Chuck Yeager's
SONIC BOOM

POP GOES THE HERO

Ever since the Wright brothers flew the first airplane in 1903 (see pages 181–185), aircraft designers had tried to get planes to go faster and faster. But what would happen if a plane tried to fly faster than the speed of sound (known as Mach 1.0)? Would it hit an air "wall" and be smashed into smithereens? Was the speed of sound some sort of outer limit of human endurance that would cause eardrums to burst and brains to literally turn to mush?

Most scientists agreed that a kind of "sound barrier" really did exist. They predicted that planes could "probably" break the sound barrier and come out safely on the other side, but there was a potential for catastrophe. Who wanted to be the pilot to test that theory?

Well, the pilot who volunteered for the job was United States Air Force Captain Chuck Yeager. A daring flight officer in the U.S. Army Air Forces during World War II, he became a test pilot after the war, trying out all kinds of experimental aircraft and rocket planes. When the National Advisory Committee for Aeronautics (NACA)—soon to have its name changed to the National Aeronautics and Space Administration (better known as NASA)—began a program to research high-speed flight, Yeager became one of its most eager pilots. In fact, two days before his historic attempt to break the sound barrier, he broke two ribs when he fell off a horse, but he was so afraid the mission would be canceled, he didn't tell anyone. He was in such pain the morning of his scheduled flight that he knew he wouldn't be able to close the hatch of his rocket-powered Bell X-1 plane, so he took a broom handle to use as a lever to seal himself inside. Then, on October 14, 1947, in the skies above California's Mojave Desert, Yeager got on board a B-29 bomber carrying the Bell X-1 underneath it. At 7,000 feet up, Yeager climbed down a ladder from the B-29 into the cockpit of the X-1 and sealed it shut (thanks to his broom handle). The B-29 continued to climb, and at 20,000 feet it released the X-1 plane. Yeager took the X-1 to 45,000 feet—and then kept increasing his speed. How fast are we talking about? About one mile in five seconds—more

The term **Mach**, used to describe the speed of objects compared to that of sound, is in honor of Ernst Mach (1838-1916), an Austrian physicist who studied optics and acoustics.

than 700 miles per hour. And when the X-1 reached the exact speed at which sound traveled at that altitude and then went faster than that speed, people on the ground miles below heard a loud "boom." It was the sound that scientists predicted would be produced if a plane went faster than Mach 1.0.

Needless to say, Yeager's plane didn't explode as it broke the sound barrier. He brought the X-1 down safely, and the crew rushed to the cockpit to see what the speed recorder registered: "Mach 1.015." Yeager wrote later that the ride had been as "smooth as a baby's bottom. Grandma could have been sitting up there sipping lemonade."

Following Yeager's successful and historic flight, the Air Force and NACA developed the second generation X-1, which flew at Mach 2—twice the speed of sound. And by 1955, planes were flying at Mach 3.

What happens after Mach 3? Did someone say Mach 4? Here's the problem. When you get to nearly four times the speed of sound, the fuselage of the plane gets so hot it's almost impossible for a person to pilot the plane, and the potential for catastrophe is extremely high for the brave people flying those planes.

The Blackbird, used by the Air Force for more than three decades, had an average speed of Mach 3.2 and could climb over 11,000 feet a minute to an altitude of 80,000 feet above the Earth. From this height, the Blackbird could survey 100,000 square miles per hour of the Earth's surface, which made it quite a handy spy plane! Even from that high up, the Blackbird could take a clear picture of a human being. Smile, you're on candid camera!

THE SCIENCE BEHIND IT

IT'S NOT SURPRISING THAT THE SOUND BARRIER fascinated and terrified people in the first half of the 20th century. The unknown can be very scary—and in the case of sound, some of the facts were hard to pin down. The exact speed of sound depends on the altitude (how high above the Earth's surface the air is). At sea level, it is 761 mph. At 30,000 feet, it is 670 mph. Why is that? Because planes, like sounds, are actually traveling through air—and air is a gas. It has weight and substance, and is capable of destroying solid objects (think of hurricanes and tornadoes). Sound travels through the air in waves: Because the air becomes less dense the higher up you go, the sound waves move more slowly than they would where the air is most dense—close to the ground. That is because the sound waves cause air molecules to vibrate, and they pass the vibrations on to other molecules—faster, if those other molecules are closer together (denser). Next time you hear the phone ring in the next room, you'll know that the sound of that ring actually traveled through the air from the phone to your ear at a rate of 761 mph.

Flight categories

Aeronautical scientists use Mach numbers (multiples of the speed of sound, abbreviated to "M") to define different types of high-speed travel—and some of the effects those speeds cause.

Subsonic (M < 1): slower than the speed of sound

Sonic (M = 1): the exact speed of sound

Transonic (0.8 < M < 1.2): travel at about the speed of sound, with some airflows greater and some less than M1

Supersonic (1.2 < M < 5): faster than the speed of sound, and the aircraft runs the risk of producing destabilizing shockwaves

Hypersonic (M > 5): very high-speed travel in which the basic chemistry of the surrounding air can be changed—and enormous heat produced

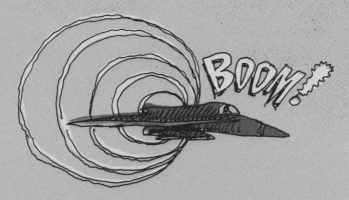

Why does the plane go "boom" once it's surpassed the speed of sound? If you try to picture waves on an ocean, you'll get the idea of how forceful waves can be when they hit—they can almost seem like solid forces. As a plane flies, it creates sound waves (sometimes called pressure waves) in all directions: These are traveling at the speed of sound. So once the plane gets closer to the speed of sound, it starts to "catch up" with the waves in front of it until it really does catch up—at Mach 1.0. At that point, as it's going past the sound/pressure waves, which form a cone behind it, it makes the sonic sound.

Even if you've never heard a plane break the sound barrier, you've almost certainly heard sonic booms. These occur naturally during an electrical storm. The flow of electrons produces a massive amount of static electricity (see pages 92–93) that we see as lightning. Lightning, of course, is not only very bright but very hot, and it heats the surrounding air very quickly. As the air warms, it expands (see pages 112–113). In this case the air expands so rapidly it's actually faster than the speed of sound, which is what makes the boom we commonly refer to as "thunder." Because light travels at a much faster speed than sound does, we actually see the flash of the lightning before we hear the crash of the thunder.

Chuck Yeager's Sonic Boom
EXPERIMENT 38

If you're wondering why all those pilots and aviation engineers were so worried about the sound barrier, try this cool demonstration of how sound waves really do have force. The sound of a human voice (shouting or even just talking) can make a mark on the sort of sensitive equipment you'll be making here.

In this experiment, you'll be creating a device that will allow you to "see" sound, or at least see how sound waves are a real, physical presence. You'll be creating a sensitive screen that can respond to outside forces by vibrating. The mirrorlike surface of the CD fragment will reflect the light while bouncing around because of the vibrations on the surface of the balloon.

This experiment can shed light on some other side effects of sound. You and your friend will be able to make the reflection jump around, thanks to the force of the sound waves. Now you can understand why people using heavy machinery wear ear protection—and why some rock musicians even lose some of their hearing.

TAKE CARE!

Take extra care breaking the CD apart (obviously making sure it's not your sister's favorite). CDs can be very sharp, and this should not be attempted without the use of goggles and adult supervision.

MATERIALS

- SCISSORS
- BALLOON
- EMPTY SOUP CAN, OPEN AT BOTH ENDS
- MASKING TAPE
- GOGGLES
- GARDENING GLOVES
- OLD CD (THAT WOULD BE THROWN OUT ANYWAY)
- GLUE
- WHITE WALL (CAN USE A BED SHEET AS A SCREEN INSTEAD)
- FLASHLIGHT
- A FRIEND

1 Use the scissors to cut off the neck of the balloon.

2 Stretch the balloon over the can so that the rubber covers one end tightly (like a drum skin).

3 Secure the edges of the balloon that are over the side of the can with masking tape all around.

4 Wearing goggles and gardening gloves, break up the CD until you get a piece that is about ¼ inch across.

5 Put a small amount of glue on the nonshiny side of this piece and press it carefully to the center of the stretched balloon.

6 Hold it in place with your finger for 30 seconds and then let the glue dry for another 3 to 4 minutes.

7 Lay the can on a table, chair, or desk with the "balloon" end pointed at the white wall or screen.

8 Shine the flashlight at the can so that the reflection of the CD mirror is reflected on the wall or screen.

9 Have a friend shout into the open end of the can and watch how the mirror reflection jumps around.

John Stapp Rides on a
ROCKET SLED

DEMONSTRATING G-FORCES—THE HARD WAY

Some scientific heroes are hardly known outside their specialty areas. One of those unsung heroes was Dr. John P. Stapp, a United States Air Force colonel who studied the effects of high speeds—and quick decelerations (slowdowns)—on human beings. Much of his research was based on his own experiences riding "rocket sleds," high-speed contraptions built on the desert floor of California. Stapp's many test runs earned him the nickname "the fastest man on Earth."

In 1946, Stapp began combining his own training as a medical doctor with

John Stapp testing the rocket sled.

enormous courage to test how people coped with extremes—of cold, heat, attitude, and pressure—firsthand. By doing this, he wanted to be able to develop protective clothing and safety features.

Some of his most influential work began in 1947 at the Aero Medical Lab at Muroc Air Force Base in California. In one test, the lab had built a 2,000-foot-long railroad line where a rocket-powered sled could reach speeds of up to 150 mph and then slow suddenly to 75 mph in just one-fifth of a second. This sudden deceleration was measured in g-forces (Gs). One G is the amount of gravitational force we feel normally. The g-forces increase as the deceleration increases. If you've ever been on a roller coaster, you probably know what that feels like.

The lab intended to use a dummy (called Oscar Eightball) to test the deceleration, but Stapp patted the dummy and said, "You can throw this away. I'm going to be the test subject." By August 1948, Stapp had gone on 16 test runs and reached speeds of 200 mph on the rocket sled,

Biomechanics: the study of how mechanical forces affect living things—or, how the living body is like a machine, with measurable limits. "Bio" comes from the Greek word *bios*, meaning "life," and "mechanics" comes from the Latin word for machine, *machina*.

subjecting himself to 35 Gs (almost twice the supposed upper limit for survival). By doing this, he was able to disprove many of the prevailing theories at the time about the limits of human endurance. He was also able to help the Air Force and United States government on a wide range of safety issues. As a pioneer in the emerging science of biomechanics, it was Stapp's studies of deceleration that

John Stapp's studies in biomechanics led to the development of pressurized spacesuits, as modeled here by test pilot Scott Crossfield in 1957.

led to the development of car seatbelts. And high-altitude pilots now have pressure suits and oxygen masks to help them cope in that punishing environment because of Stapp's daring experiments.

Although Stapp spent much of his life placing himself in harm's way in the name of science—talk about potential catastrophe!—he managed to live until the ripe old age of 89.

THE SCIENCE BEHIND IT

DR. STAPP SPENT HIS PROFESSIONAL CAREER specializing in biomechanics. At its most basic level, biomechanics is about applying mechanical principles to living things. We see this often in the area of sports, for instance. People are always coming up with new and improved racquets for tennis, more aerodynamic helmets for bicyclists, more streamlined bathing suits for speed swimmers. A baseball team might hire a specialist to study a pitcher's delivery to see whether he can develop a better curve ball or add 5 mph to his fastball. All these mechanical advancements give players more power and better control at the same time without calling for extra effort on the part of the players. And it's all a product of biomechanics.

An expert in biomechanics must consider Newton's Laws of Motion (see page 83) and the forces associated with them to see how the human body will be affected by specific actions. Among those are centripetal force (which draws objects traveling on a curved path toward the center), potential energy (energy that is built up and stored), and kinetic energy (the energy that something has because of its movement).

Centripetal Force

Potential Energy

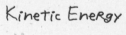

Kinetic Energy

John Stapp's Rocket Sled
EXPERIMENT 39

This experiment captures the spirit of Dr. Stapp, who managed to keep his sense of fun—and a sense of humor—throughout his career. It's also a great excuse to get your parents to take you to the amusement park, and while you're there you can imagine yourself as a test subject.

MATERIALS

- AMUSEMENT PARK (WITH RIDES)
- NOTEBOOK
- PENCIL

TAKE CARE!

Leave your pencil and notebook with someone as you go on each ride. You don't want to lose your valuable research if you're upside down on a loop rollercoaster.

1 Remember that you're going on these rides in the cause of science, not just for fun. Right?

2 First take a spin on the bumper cars. The movement of the cars is an excellent demonstration of kinetic energy. And if you crash? That's a bonus, because you've just experienced Newton's first law of motion—the other car was the "outside force" that altered your movement!

3 Now buy a ticket for the roller coaster. Even as you wait and listen to the screams, you can tell that you're going to be in for some more kinetic energy. But the target here is to identify the potential energy—which builds and builds and builds as the cars slowly climb that first hill.

4 The third ride that you need to test is the Tilt-a-Whirl. As it gains speed, you'll feel pressed hard against the frame of the ride. People often describe this as demonstrating your body's *outward* centrifugal force. In reality it's the ride's *inward* centripetal force that's at work: Your body really wants to go shooting off in a straight line.

John Stapp's Deceleration
EXPERIMENT 40

This experiment demonstrates deceleration: If you increase the amount of time needed to stop a moving object, you'll need less force to do so. Here you'll be throwing an egg as hard as you can at an object—but the egg won't break. Why? Because you're giving the egg a little extra time to hit—even if it's only an extra 10th of a second or so—by using the sheet. Think of a car approaching a red light. The driver could simply tap the brakes gently for perhaps 10 seconds, or jam them on hard at the last instant. Which do you think needs more energy?

MATERIALS

- TWO VOLUNTEERS
- BED SHEET
- EGG
- GOLF BALL (OPTIONAL)

TAKE CARE!

There's no need to remind anyone about the consequences of breaking an egg on a freshly cleaned sheet. You needn't really worry about that, but if you're feeling a little edgy, you can practice a few times using a golf ball instead of an egg. Which comes with its own warning: Don't do it anywhere near a window.

1 Have your volunteers hold the sheet so there is enough slack to make a trough.

2 Stand about 10 feet from the sheet, pick up the egg, and take aim at the trough of the sheet.

3 Throw the egg as hard as you can.

4 The egg shouldn't break.

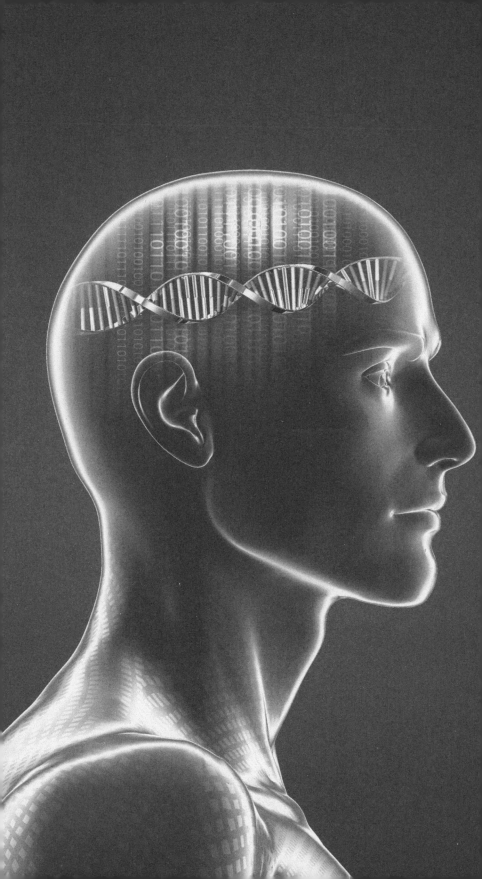

Watson and Crick's
DNA

DID SOMEONE SAY "BRAVE NEW WORLD"?

Eagle Pub stands next to the dormitories of Corpus Christi, one of the colleges that make up Cambridge University in England. It's the sort of place where people quietly sip their tea beside a welcoming fire. So you can imagine the startled reaction on the regulars' faces at lunchtime on February 28, 1953, when two young men burst through the door and into the pub. They must have been even more surprised when one of the men exclaimed: "We have discovered the secret of life."

James D. Watson (born 1928) was a child prodigy, enrolling at the University of Chicago at the age of 15. He later became a molecular biologist.

Francis Crick (1916–2004) was originally interested in a career in physics, but turned to molecular biology after serving in WW II. (He designed a minesweeper that was instrumental in protecting British ships from German mines.)

That young man, Francis Crick, was telling the truth—certainly he and his friend James Watson had discovered *a* secret of life. They had cracked a natural code that lay behind one of the great scientific mysteries: Just how do living things reproduce themselves? Scientists and the general public had long known about eggs and seeds in animals and plants, but no one could explain exactly how it was that blue-eyed people often had blue-eyed children, or how some families are better than others at sports, or art, or business.

Watson and Crick had unraveled the secrets behind deoxyribonucleic acid (DNA), the substance inside every living organism that contains its genetic blueprint. This discovery opened up all sorts of possibilities in the world of medicine (doctors might be able to identify and cure genetic illnesses), farming (crops and animals could be bred to become bigger or more nourishing), and even crime prevention (everyone's DNA is different, making it even more precise an identifier than a fingerprint). The scientific world recognized Watson and Crick's accomplishment by awarding them the Nobel Prize in Medicine in 1962.

Not everyone was—or is—happy with the arrival of DNA information on the scene. Some people worry that tinkering with the genes of plants and animals—and eventually humans—can lead us down a slippery ethical slope that can only end in catastrophe. What if, for instance, parents could choose the sex of their children ahead of time? Would the world eventually have far fewer women than men? What if a person's height or eye color could be predetermined before he/she is born? Could DNA be used to create a race of "super" humans—faster, stronger, smarter—than ordinary people born the old-fashioned way? It all starts to sound a bit like science fiction—until you see a picture of a liger. That's when you start to feel like the novel *Brave New World*'s vision isn't so far away after all.

A **liger** is a hybrid "super" cat created by crossing a male lion with a tigress. At 10 to 12 feet long, weighing as much as both parents together, a liger is the world's largest cat.

THE SCIENCE BEHIND IT

BY THE 1950S, THE SCIENTIFIC WORLD KNEW THAT inside every cell of every living thing were genes, which contained sets of instructions to be passed on to offspring (such as blue eyes or left-handedness). People even knew that these genes were linked together in strands called chromosomes. The real question was what held chromosomes together—and how did they allow traits to be passed on?

The scientific detective trail led to the discovery of the chemical substance called deoxyribonucleic acid (DNA), which acts as a sort of glue to hold chromosomes together. DNA was discovered before Watson and Crick "discovered the secret of life," but no one could be sure just how chromosomes (and their DNA) managed to copy information about genes and reproduce that information in a new organism.

Watson and Crick, working at the Cavendish Laboratory in Cambridge (the Eagle was a favorite pub for Cavendish staff), focused on the shape of DNA. They were working on a couple of leads in their research. The first was an observation by Erwin Chargaff, of Columbia University, that DNA's complicated chemical makeup had a number of patterns repeating themselves. The second was even more dramatic—a special X-ray photograph (known as "photo 51") taken by Rosalind Franklin of King's College London that helped point Watson and Crick in the right direction. DNA, they realized, consisted of two "spiraling" strands that form a double helix shape. Each strand carries genetic information that is paired with and connects with the other strand.

Understanding the shape was a crucial breakthrough, but seeing what happened next was truly groundbreaking. Watson and Crick observed that the DNA strands could "unzip" during cell division (part of the reproduction process), with a new strand—copied exactly like the one that had peeled off—in its place. This process continues, with the genetic information being passed on to each new set of DNA.

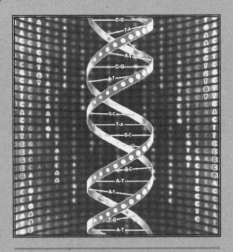

Sometimes the DNA gets it wrong and doesn't make an exact copy. Such a mistake is called a mutation.

Recognizing the double helix shape was vital to Watson and Crick's understanding of how genetic information was stored—and passed on—in living things.

Remember, though, that many mutations are actually helpful—Charles Darwin noted how they lay at the heart of natural selection (see pages 156–157). Scientists can also introduce mutations by adding different DNA to the cells. While this kind of genetic engineering has led to the creation of the liger and other hybrid animals, it has also had more useful applications in the agriculture and health industries. Plants can now be engineered to survive in freezing temperatures, making them easier to grow. And people with rare genetic disorders have a shot at getting treated or even cured with human gene therapy.

Watson and Crick's DNA
EXPERIMENT 41

Every living thing has its own DNA "signature," a chemical "blueprint" that makes it different from every other living thing. People leave traces of their DNA on things they touch or eat, and since no two people have the same exact combination of genes, DNA evidence has become a crucial part of criminal investigations. The following experiment shows you how it works. You will be extracting DNA from an ordinary banana. DNA, like other chemicals, is stored inside cells. By placing the banana in a food processor, you will be breaking down some of the cell walls that lock the DNA inside the cells. The dishwashing liquid you will be adding contains soap molecules to dissolve the plasma membranes and nuclear membranes, helping to release the DNA. Finally, by adding alcohol, you help separate the DNA (which the alcohol draws out of the water through dehydration) from other proteins and grease (which do dissolve in water). The fluffy material at the end of the experiment is DNA that did not dissolve in the alcohol. Don't forget, though: *Seeing* a whole load of DNA is one thing, but seeing inside it to learn how it works is quite another, and that's how Watson and Crick won the Nobel Prize.

MATERIALS

- HALF-EATEN BANANA
- FOOD PROCESSOR
- SALT
- CUP
- HOT WATER
- SIEVE
- TEASPOON
- DISHWASHING LIQUID
- PAPER COFFEE FILTER
- CLEAR DRINKING GLASS
- DENATURED ALCOHOL
- WOODEN SKEWER

TAKE CARE!
Make sure that an adult handles and pours the denatured alcohol and then disposes of it afterward.

1 Put the banana into the food processor.

2 Add a teaspoon of salt to half a cup of hot water.

3 Pour the saltwater mixture in with the banana and process for 1 minute. Rinse the spoon and cup.

4 Pour the mixture through a sieve back into the cup. Press the back of the spoon against the sieve to push the solids through.

5 Add a teaspoon of dishwashing liquid. Stir occasionally for 5 minutes.

6 Set the coffee filter over the drinking glass and pour the mixture into it, so that it drips into the glass.

7 Slowly pour denatured alcohol down the side of the glass until it forms a half-inch layer on the top of the mixture.

8 A layer of stringy white material (with bubbles attached to it)—the DNA—should form between the mixture and the denatured alcohol. Some people describe it as looking "snotty," but that's not a scientific term, is it?

9 Slowly twist the wooden skewer inside the substance to extract some of this DNA.

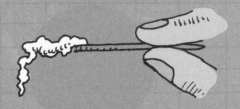

Theodore Maiman's LASER BEAM

THE "KILLER RAY GUN" OF SCI-FI NIGHTMARES?

It is still a matter of wonder how the Martians are able to slay men so swiftly and so silently. Many think that in some way they are able to generate an intense heat which they project in a parallel beam against any object they choose, by means of a polished parabolic mirror of unknown composition, much as the parabolic mirror of a lighthouse projects a beam of light."

Those are the words of British author H. G. Wells in his famous novel *War of the Worlds*, which is about a Martian invasion of Earth. Wells wrote his book in 1898; 40 years later Orson Welles terrified

American radio listeners with a broadcast of the same story—this time transferring the invasion from England to New Jersey.

One of the most unsettling elements of that fictional Martian invasion was the killer ray gun (Wells called it a "Heat-Ray"), which could burn through anything that became its target. Wells seemed to have hit on something that could terrify people: the idea of concentrating light into a single, focused beam of enormous power. But such a beam wasn't just the product of a novelist's imagination: Theodore Maiman, a scientist at Hughes Electric Corporation in California, was working to produce just such a beam in real life, even if he had no plans to invade any other planets with it.

When CBS Radio aired Welles's dramatized version of War of the Worlds, thousands of people panicked, believing that CBS was reporting a real Martian invasion.

Most of the research in the 1950s had focused on radio waves, not light beams. In 1954, Charles Townes and Arthur Schawlow had invented a device to amplify—or strengthen—microwaves, which are a type of electromagnetic radiation with wavelengths just shorter than those of FM radio waves. This tool for studying distant objects in outer space was called the maser (Microwave Amplification by Stimulated Emission of Radiation). The waves sent out by masers could amplify the electromagnetic waves that they passed through, making it easier to identify what was creating that distant radiation. The laser (Light Amplification by Stimulated Emission of Radiation) went one step further. Instead of microwaves, it emitted a beam of light.

Because of their strength and concentrated beams, lasers can be put to all sorts of uses. Medical lasers make it easier for surgeons to perform delicate operations; patients feel less pain because there's less cutting involved. Doctors use lasers to treat eye injuries, smooth out wrinkles, remove birthmarks, and even treat acne. CDs, DVDs, and supermarket bar codes all work with laser technology. Powerful lasers are used in all sorts of manufacturing processes.

All of these advantages, however, can be turned on their head catastrophically if the lasers are used for bad things. Something that can burn through metal (to produce an automobile) could theoretically be turned into a powerful weapon. It may sound like something out of *Star Trek*, but the potential is there. Beam me up, Scotty! Or rather, set your lasers to "stun."

THE SCIENCE BEHIND IT

THE IDEA OF HARNESSING THE ENERGY OF RADIA-
tion and focusing it to make it even more powerful
didn't just blossom in the 20th century. For centuries, people had been aware that the Sun's rays, for
example, could be directed into a beam that would
be hot enough to burn objects. In 212 B.C., the
Greek inventor Archimedes was said to have built a
"burning mirror," which directed the Sun's rays and
destroyed an entire Roman fleet.

Illustration of Archimedes' "burning mirror": an ancient laser beam?

Whether or not the burning mirror really did exist,
later observers noted that lenses could also focus the
rays of the Sun: For example, a magnifying glass can
be used to burn a hole through paper.

It isn't surprising that authors as well as scientists
in the early 20th century would look for new technologies to create even more power and heat. And
the starting point for laser development came in

Maiman's Laser

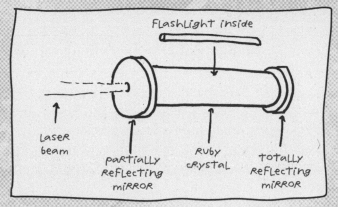

1917, in a paper written by Albert Einstein. This paper outlined the first step—which appears in the abbreviations "maser" and "laser" and in the words "stimulated emission."

Stimulated emission is when a particle of light, called a photon, hits an electron (one of the tiny subparticles in atoms), causing it to produce another photon. The result is two photons where there had been one. The process can be continued so that more and more photons are produced in a process a bit like that of a chain reaction (see page 218).

Theodore Maiman's breakthrough came when he flashed white light into a cylinder made of ruby. This was the "stimulated emission" stage. Blue and green wavelengths of light were absorbed, while the red wavelength was made much stronger (amplified). As the emission continued, loads of photons were building up inside the cylinder, moving around like crazy. Maiman put a fully reflective mirror at one end of the cylinder to reflect these photons back inside, and another not-quite-fully reflective mirror at the opposite end. The concentrated flow of photons poured out through that opening in a narrow beam—a laser beam.

Theodore Maiman's Laser Oven
EXPERIMENT 42

This experiment is a cool (er, *hot*) demonstration of the same principles at work behind a laser beam. Your handmade oven works by focusing the Sun's rays toward the food tray. The foil increases the number of rays entering the oven. They can pass through the plastic, but the heat stays inside. The result—evidence you can eat.

MATERIALS

- A LARGE PIZZA BOX (THE SORT YOU GET WHEN YOU ORDER A LARGE TAKEOUT PIZZA)
- RULER
- FELT-TIP PEN
- SCISSORS
- ALUMINUM FOIL
- NONTOXIC GLUE
- 8¹/₂-INCH X 11-INCH SHEET OF STURDY CLEAR PLASTIC (PREFERABLY LAMINATED)
- DUCT TAPE
- BLACK CONSTRUCTION PAPER

TAKE CARE!

Bear in mind that you have actually constructed an oven, which can reach temperatures of up to 270 degrees Fahrenheit. But it takes its time to reach that temperature. Leave half an hour for the oven to preheat, and then figure on cooking things for twice as long as you would in a normal oven.

1 Draw a box on the top flap of the pizza box, about 1 to 2 inches in from the edge.

2 Carefully cut along 3 of those 4 lines, leaving the line along the "hinge" of the box alone. Open and close several times to form a crease.

3 Cut a piece of foil the same size as this flap; glue it to the inside (lower) edge of the flap.

CATASTROPHE METER : **INVOLVES USE OF HOT SURFACES AND SHARP OBJECTS**

4 Measure and cut a piece of plastic just a bit larger than the opening; tape this plastic to the underside of the box top, making sure it covers the cutout hole to form a complete air seal. At this point, the box top should have this new plastic seal on the underside; the foil-backed flap opens up from this plastic layer.

5 Cut a second piece of foil and glue it to the bottom (inside) of the pizza box.

6 Cut some of the black construction paper to fit this same base; tape it on top of the foil on the base. The now-covered foil will work as a heat insulator rather than as a reflector.

7 Aim the box so that it opens toward the Sun.

8 Prop the flap open—but with the box top shut—to get the oven working.

9 You can cook all sorts of things—English muffins, s'mores, and maybe even more pizza—provided they don't protrude higher than the box top.

Theodore Maiman's Flashlight Beam
EXPERIMENT 43

This experiment is a great way to learn about why lasers are so different from ordinary light sources. A single laser beam aimed from the Earth would still be visible on the Moon. Its beam would have diverged (spread out, as all light eventually does) so that it would be spread across half a mile on the lunar surface. Still—only half a mile after traveling more than 240,000 miles. Not bad, really! To put that in perspective, this experiment gives you a chance to measure how much the beam from an ordinary flashlight diverges and dims over a *much* smaller distance. It works best if you do this experiment in a darkened room.

MATERIALS

- **RULER**
- **NOTEBOOK**
- **1 SHEET OF BLANK 8½-INCH X 11-INCH PAPER**
- **TAPE**
- **TABLE**
- **ONE TEXTBOOK (ABOUT 2-INCH THICK)**
- **SMALL FLASHLIGHT (WITH A TIGHT BEAM)**
- **PINK, YELLOW, BLUE, AND GREEN HIGHLIGHTERS**

TAKE CARE!
Never shine a flashlight in anyone's eyes.

1 Use the ruler to mark a vertical line 2 inches from the left edge of the paper. Continue drawing vertical lines every 2 inches. It should look like this:

2 Tape that sheet of paper to the tabletop.

3 Place the textbook on the sheet of paper, aligning its spine with the first line you drew on the paper.

4 Rest the flashlight across the top of the textbook so that its beam faces the left edge of the paper.

5 Turn the flashlight on. Turn off any other lights in the room.

6 Measure how wide the circle of light is by tracing the edge of the light on the paper with the pink highlighter.

7 Slide the textbook back so that it now aligns with the second line you drew on the paper. This time use the yellow highlighter to measure the width of the circle of light.

8 Slide the textbook back two more times using the other two highlighters.

9 You will see that the circle of light becomes larger—and dimmer—as the distance becomes greater.

10 Try to predict when the circle would become invisible. Is it less than 240,000 miles?

Yuri Gagarin
GOES INTO ORBIT

AND IT'S "OUT OF THIS WORLD"

Almost as soon as World War II ended in 1945, another war began, with the United States opposing the Soviet Union. This "cold war" wasn't really a war in the normal sense: American soldiers never went to fight Russian soldiers directly. Instead, it was fought indirectly—and it was a race to get the biggest, baddest weapons in their stockpile.

But even though no shots were ever fired between the two enemies, both countries—and the wider world—lived in fear. What would happen, for example, if a trigger-happy American pilot shot down a Russian plane? Or if the Russians fired on an American submarine off their shore? Would it lead to another world war? Ever since the atom bomb was dropped on Hiroshima, people knew that the consequences of another world war could be catastrophic for the entire world—could even wipe out the human race.

One of the things that stopped war from breaking out was the balance of weapons between the countries. Both the United States and the Soviet Union had many atomic bombs (see pages 218–221)—and both wanted to create weapons the other didn't have. They were each looking for an advantage that could give them the technological edge over the other.

That was when people began looking up to the skies. The United States and the Soviet Union had already been building rockets that could send weapons thousands of miles (see page 264). What would happen if one of them were able to launch a vehicle into outer space, or from outer space, or through outer space? The race was on to get human beings in space, and in November 1957, it seemed that the Soviet Union would win that race when it launched the first satellite, Sputnik. A month later they sent a second Sputnik into space—this time with a dog named Laika on board. Could a human be far behind?

A **satellite** is any object that revolves around another object (especially planet) in outer space. Satellites can be natural (like the Moon) or artificial (manmade objects such as communications satellites or the International Space Station).

As the United States scrambled to catch up in the "space race," the Soviet Union shocked the world again when, on April 12, 1961, it put a man into orbit around the Earth—and brought him down safely again. That cosmonaut (the Russian term for astronaut) was Yuri Gagarin, and he became a national hero.

The United States saw Gagarin's triumphant space flight as the ultimate challenge. On May 25, 1961, President John F. Kennedy promised to put an American astronaut on the Moon "before this decade [the 1960s] is out." One of the problems, however, was that the Americans hadn't yet developed the rocket power to do that. Their rockets still lacked the power (thrust) to go up fast enough to break free of the atmosphere and go into orbit around the Earth. So the Americans went into overdrive. They concentrated on producing a type of rocket that could power heavy payloads into orbit—and possibly beyond. These Saturn rockets were the key to the American space program in the 1960s.

All that hard work paid off, of course, because on July 20, 1969, American astronauts Neil Armstrong and Edwin "Buzz" Aldrin became the first human beings to land on the Moon.

The Soviet government banned Gagarin from making any other space flights because it didn't want such a national hero to die in an accident. Unfortunately, that is exactly what happened in 1968: Gagarin died not in a spacecraft but on a normal flight in his new role as a flying instructor.

THE SCIENCE BEHIND IT

ALTHOUGH THE COLD WAR LED TO THE ARMS RACE, and the arms race led to the space race, and people lived in fear of the catastrophes that could arise if the Cold War between the United States and the Soviets ever became a real war, diplomacy, time, and a little luck worked in everyone's favor. Several treaties were signed to stop the proliferation of nuclear weapons and to even reduce the size of the stockpiles that existed. In 1991, the Soviet government crumbled—and just like smoke, the threat that had loomed since the Cold War vanished. Nowadays, American and Russian astronauts join forces on space missions—and there's even an International Space Station manned by both astronauts and cosmonauts.

Although the "end of the world" catastrophe never happened, there is no avoiding the fact that every space mission is risky, and Gagarin's was probably the riskiest of all because he was venturing into the unknown.

The science behind rockets had been developing for many centuries, starting with the Chinese (see pages 53–57) right through to the work of Robert Goddard (see pages 199–203). By the 20th century, scientists had an excellent awareness of how objects move on Earth—and what it takes to help them travel away from Earth.

The Saturn V rocket, standing 363 feet tall, had enough power to send American astronauts nearly 240,000 miles across space to the Moon in 1969—and back again safely. The first (lowest) stage of the

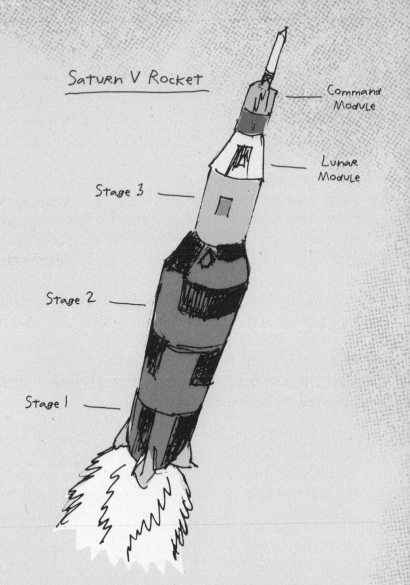

Saturn V Rocket

Command Module

Lunar Module

Stage 3

Stage 2

Stage 1

rocket took it to a height of 38 miles and a speed of 6,000 mph. Burning for just two minutes, its five engines consumed nearly 4.5 million pounds of fuel. The second stage consumed another million pounds of fuel to reach a height of 118 miles and a speed of 14,000 mph. The third stage of the Saturn fired twice: first to reach the orbital speed of 17,400 mph and again to power the three-man *Apollo* spacecraft out of Earth's orbit and on the way to the Moon.

Gagarin's Orbit
EXPERIMENT 44

This experiment gives you an idea of the sorts of problems that rocket scientists face when they launch a fast-moving rocket from a spinning object such as Earth. It's not as easy as you might think . . . as you'll soon find out after a few tosses at your local playground.

MATERIALS

- **PLAYGROUND MERRY-GO-ROUND:** THE SORT THAT YOU PUSH AND RIDE
- **10 BALLS (TENNIS BALLS, BASEBALLS, SOFTBALLS—ANYTHING THAT YOU CAN THROW)**
- **A ROUND BASKET**
- **SHOPPING BAG**
- **A FRIEND OR TWO**

TAKE CARE!
Make sure there's no one in the firing line as you start tossing balls from the spinning merry-go-round.

1 Set the empty basket about five paces from the edge of the merry-go-round.

2 Pile the balls into the shopping bag and set the shopping bag at the center of the merry-go-round.

3 Climb onto the motionless merry-go-round at the closest point to the basket.

4 One by one, throw the balls into the basket on the side of the merry-go-round. See how many "baskets" you can score.

5 Now, pack the balls into the shopping bag again and once more set it in the middle of the merry-go-round.

6 Start pushing the merry-go-round until it is moving pretty well, and hop on.

7 How many baskets can you score now? It will be quite a feat if you can score even one in the basket! The challenge you've just faced is the same problem rocket scientists had to tackle when they were trying to figure out how to launch a spaceship from the spinning Earth—except the Earth is spinning at about 1,000 mph!

Gagarin's Balloon Thrust
EXPERIMENT 45

The key to getting a rocket to leave the atmosphere and go into orbit is thrust, the power needed to give it that essential speed. And in order to achieve that sort of power, you need to have a reliable fuel supply—and enough of it.

This experiment uses balloons to help you make the connection between fuel, thrust, length of flight, and the distance covered. Basically, you're the one supplying the fuel (with your breaths), which in turn determines the amount of thrust that your balloon rockets will have. Then you can see the direct relationship between thrust and the length of the flight.

MATERIALS

- BALLOONS OF DIFFERENT SIZES (LIKE THE "PARTY BAG" OF BALLOONS)
- PENCIL
- PAPER
- AT LEAST ONE FRIEND TO HELP
- STOPWATCH OR WATCH WITH A SECOND HAND
- RULER OR TAPE MEASURE
- GRAPH PAPER (OPTIONAL)

TAKE CARE!

This experiment works best if you have a lot of room—you really do want the balloons to cover a lot of distance. But be careful if it is too windy, because a sudden gust could throw your calculations off.

1 Choose about 4 or 5 balloons of different sizes and record them as "1" to "4" (or "5") on your paper. Leave a good bit of space between each balloon entry, because you'll be adding more information.

2 For each balloon entry, mark "Size," "Length of Flight," and "Distance."

3 Blow up a balloon using a series of same-size breaths: Have your friend count those breaths and mark them under "Size."

4 Pinch the balloon shut and take it to the launch site.

5 Have your friend get ready to time the flight from the moment you let go.

6 Keeping the pinched end pointing at you, hold the balloon out and let go.

7 Ask your friend to mark the time under "Length of Flight," and then you can both measure the distance it flew and enter that under "Distance."

8 Repeat steps 3 to 7 for each balloon.

9 See whether you can draw any conclusions between the size of the balloon's fuel supply (the number of breaths) and the time and distance.

10 If you want, you can make charts of these relationships using "Number of Breaths" as the Y axis (the upward-pointing one) and "Length of Flight" and then "Distance" for the horizontal X axis.

Rachel Carson's
SILENT SPRING

DEATH OF OUR NATIONAL SYMBOL?

It was common in the 1950s to see small trucks driving slowly along suburban streets, across farms, and even on beaches shooting out powerful sprays, like giant garden hoses. The spray contained DDT, one of the most successful pesticides ever produced, and it was used to kill mosquitoes, gypsy moths, and other troublesome insects.

DDT (or dichloro-diphenyl-trichloro-ethane, if you really want to impress your friends) was developed in 1874, but its success in killing insects wasn't recognized until 1939—and it was kept secret at first.

The public didn't learn about this "miracle pesticide" until 1944, when the U.S. Army and other government departments released information about how effective it was. Before that, news about DDT had been censored—it was so powerful that some people obviously considered it to be almost a secret weapon.

The June 12, 1944, issue of *Time* magazine spelled out some of the amazing results achieved with DDT:

- When sprayed on a wall, it kills any flies that touch the surface for up to three months.

- Clothing dusted with DDT is free of lice, even after eight washings.

- A few ounces dropped in a swamp kill all mosquito larvae.

- It kills household pests such as cockroaches, moths, termites, and dog's fleas.

Such a chemical could almost be described as a "wonder drug" because mosquitoes and other insects weren't just pests: They spread deadly diseases such as malaria and typhus. It seemed too good to be true that a simple spray could wipe out the transmitters of these diseases. Unfortunately, it *was* too good to be true.

During the 1950s, when DDT use was at its peak, a young woman named Rachel Carson started noticing things that she began to link to the powerful insecticide. She was trained as a marine biologist (someone who studies water-based life) and also produced publications for the U.S. Fish and Wildlife Service. She heard about—and also observed firsthand—dead fish floating on lakes and a strange quiet in places that were once loud with bird song. In 1958, she learned from a friend on Cape Cod, Massachusetts, that seabirds were also dying mysteriously. Worse still, the bald eagle—America's national symbol—was in danger of becoming extinct in much of the country.

That news prompted Carlson into action, and she put her two skills—science and writing—to work. Over the next four years, she researched and wrote a book that gave scientific evidence that chemicals —especially DDT—were responsible for this widespread destruction of wildlife. The book, entitled *Silent Spring*, was published in 1962. The title referred to what would happen if people continued to pump chemicals into the environment.

Silent Spring caused an immediate outcry. It became a bestseller and people began to take note of the damage caused by overuse of chemicals.

Carson's tireless work is all the more remarkable because she was suffering from breast cancer and must have been in terrible pain. She would die from that disease in 1964, just two years after the publication of her groundbreaking book. But she had planted some seeds that would grow for decades. The world became aware—almost overnight—of the environment, and governments began to take urgent measures to reverse the damage.

One of those measures was the U.S. decision to ban DDT in 1972 and to investigate the effects of dozens of other chemicals that were once used freely.

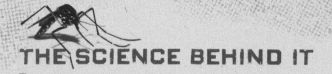

THE SCIENCE BEHIND IT

Rachel Carson's position as a scientist within the U.S. Fish and Wildlife Service gave her an excellent chance to work out what was happening to America's wildlife, why it was happening, and where it would all lead.

First of all, she understood the basic chemistry that made DDT so successful as an insecticide. It gets inside the inner workings of the insect's cells and causes the nervous system to get confused and send out wrong signals. DDT does this because it dissolves in fat, and the outer layer of any animal cell is made up of fat. As the DDT works its way into each cell, it also "leaves the door open" for other chemicals to get inside. These chemicals, forms of the elements potassium and sodium, are the ones that jumble up the signals that the insect's nervous system sends out. The result is that it dies, either from convulsions (uncontrolled movement) or paralysis (inability to move).

Larva: the newly hatched phase of mosquitoes and other insects when they look like worms and have no wings. The plural is "larvae."

Much of this chemical damage is done when the mosquitoes are in the early larva stage of their lives. But the wider damage—to other species and to the environment generally—continues, and even grows. Once the DDT finds its way into the mosquito's fatty cell membranes, it stays there. Then, when another animal eats that mosquito, the DDT passes into *its* fatty tissue. But birds, for example, don't limit themselves to one insect per day: they eat *thousands*, and all that DDT builds up.

The Food Chain

This term describes the natural balance among the organisms in a particular area (called a habitat). In particular, it describes the eating relationships between different species and how, ultimately, they all depend on each other. For example, a forest food chain would begin with grass or shrubs. Plant-eaters such as mice, deer, and rabbits eat them, and these animals in turn are eaten by predators such as owls, lynx, wolves, and bears. Scavengers such as buzzards eat dead animals, and decomposers such as insects and fungi break up the waste.

Insects and birds are just two elements in the wider food chain, which connects all the living organisms in a location. Birds get eaten by bigger birds, such as hawks; other birds (like the bald eagle) eat fish that have also collected DDT. Then some of the meat-eaters get eaten by bigger meat-eaters, like bears and wolves.

The DDT that these animals collect does not kill them outright. Instead, it works in other ways. The chemical damages the way many birds produce calcium to harden the shells of their eggs, causing the eggs to crack when the mother rests on them in the nest. Pelicans, robins, and bald eagles all suffered in this way because of DDT.

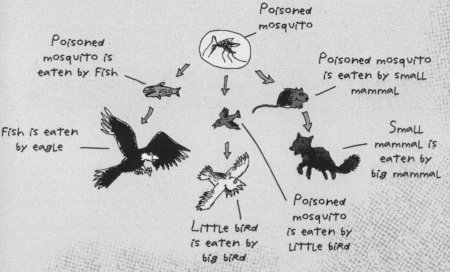

Poisoned mosquito

Poisoned mosquito is eaten by Fish

Poisoned mosquito is eaten by small mammal

Fish is eaten by eagle

Small mammal is eaten by big mammal

Poisoned mosquito is eaten by Little bird

Little bird is eaten by big bird

Rachel Carson's Clean Water
EXPERIMENT 46

Thanks to Rachel Carson and other activists, people are taking much more interest in protecting the environment. Banning DDT and other harmful chemicals, as well as controlling the amount of waste entering the air and water, has had an enormous effect. Many habitats have seen a return of plant and animal species that had been missing for decades. The numbers of walleye, an important food fish, are thriving once more in Lake Erie, which was always considered to be the most polluted Great Lake. And wild salmon have even begun swimming up the River Seine into Paris.

Those success stories are good examples of how nature can solve problems, if it is given a chance. As long as the flow of waste materials and pollutants is reduced or stopped, water can often clean itself.

This experiment shows how the water cycle—the constant cycle of evaporation (liquid water turning into water vapor, a gas) and condensation (the vapor cooling into liquid form again)—helps separate water from other materials. It works best on a warm, sunny day.

MATERIALS

- MEASURING CUP
- DIRT OR SAND
- MIXING BOWL (ABOUT 8-INCH DIAMETER)
- WATER
- MIXING SPOON
- CLEAR DRINKING GLASS (LESS THAN HALF AS HIGH AS THE MIXING BOWL)
- PLASTIC WRAP
- A PLAYING MARBLE

TAKE CARE!
Some people find it a bit tricky getting the plastic wrap slack over the bowl but tight around the rim. Make sure you have enough plastic wrap so that you can have two or three goes to get it right.

1 Mix 2 cups of dirt or sand with 2 pints of water in the mixing bowl. Stir the mixture well.

2 Carefully put the drinking glass in the center of the bowl, easing it into the mixture but not letting the mixture into it.

3 Cut a length of plastic wrap about as long as it is wide, so that you have roughly a square shape.

4 Put the wrap over the opening of the bowl, but not too tightly. You must leave some slack.

5 Put the bowl in a sunny position, either by a window or outside, and place the marble on the wrap directly above the glass. (Because of the slack, the marble should rest neatly above it, enabling water to drip from it straight into the glass later in the experiment.)

6 Leave for several hours and then peel off the plastic wrap.

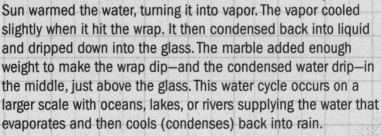

7 You should find some clean water inside the glass and the sand or dirt mixture much drier. That is because the Sun warmed the water, turning it into vapor. The vapor cooled slightly when it hit the wrap. It then condensed back into liquid and dripped down into the glass. The marble added enough weight to make the wrap dip—and the condensed water drip—in the middle, just above the glass. This water cycle occurs on a larger scale with oceans, lakes, or rivers supplying the water that evaporates and then cools (condenses) back into rain.

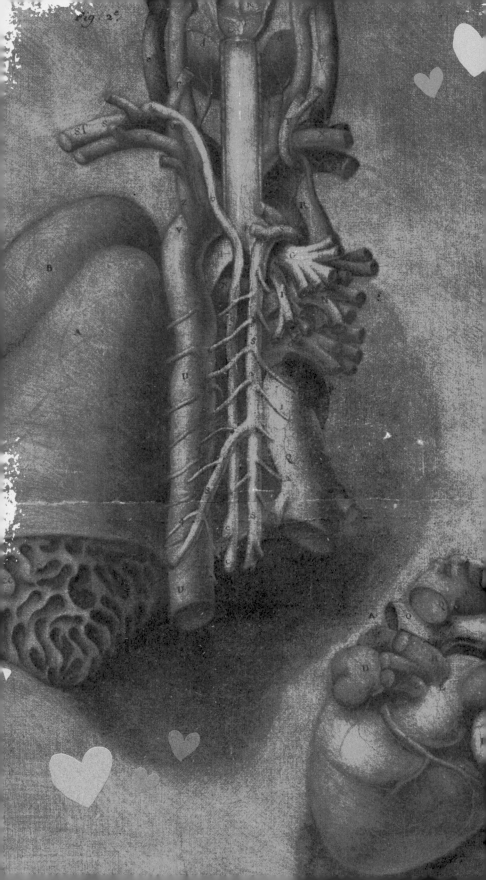

Christiaan Barnard's HUMAN HEART TRANSPLANT

THOSE FRANKENSTEIN FEARS ARE GROWING . . .

Before the middle of the 20th century, the idea of removing a human organ (such as a kidney, liver, or heart) and replacing it with one from a dead person was the stuff of dreams—or nightmares. For many people, it conjured up images of grave robbers at work in shadowy cemeteries on moonless nights. Probably the most famous of these nightmarish transplants were those that gave life to Frankenstein's monster, in Mary Shelley's famous novel of 1818.

Others viewed such operations as lifesavers. After all, a dead person isn't going to need his or her liver or heart anymore, and if transplanting it to a sick person saves that person's life, then where's the problem? In fact, there were several problems standing in the way of organ transplants—some were medical and others went far beyond medical science and into the realm of ethics.

By the early 20th century, doctors were on the threshold of breakthroughs in organ transplants. New surgical techniques and medicines made them confident that a transplanted organ could work in its new home. Meanwhile they dealt with the sensitive issue of right and wrong by focusing on the lives that could be saved or prolonged if patients received transplanted organs.

And they tackled the "grave-robbing" accusation head-on: Rather than stealing organs from corpses, medical staff would ask people for permission (or consent) in their lifetime. Today it has become common for people to carry identification alerting medical staff that they are willing to offer their organs for transplant in case they die. In the 1950s and early 1960s, doctors usually had to approach the surviving family members of people who had just died.

In 1954, doctors in Boston performed the first kidney transplant, using a kidney from a living donor. Eight years later the same team transplanted a kidney from a person who had just died. Lung and liver transplants followed in 1963 and 1967.

On December 3, 1967, Doctor Christiaan Barnard performed the first human heart transplant, in Cape Town, South Africa. Louis Washkansky was a 55-year-old dying of heart disease. In a nine-hour

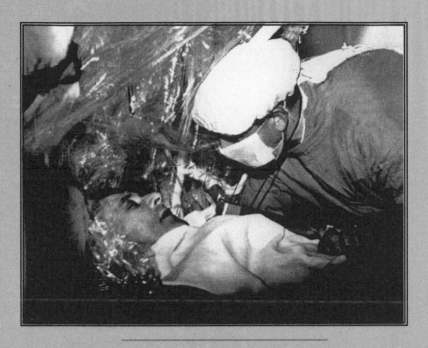

Dr. Barnard checking on his patient after performing a human heart transplant.

operation, Barnard removed the heart of a 25-year-old woman who had died in an auto accident and placed it in Washkansky's chest. The operation was a success, but the medicine that Washkansky took to combat rejection (see "The Science Behind It" on page 282) left him open to infection. Only 18 days after he had the operation, Washkansky died of pneumonia. However, he knew he would have died without the operation. And he knew that the medical world would benefit from his experience, no matter how potentially catastrophic the surgery proved to be. That hope was fulfilled: Advances in surgical techniques and antirejection medicines have meant that patients can now live for years or even decades with a new heart. Thank you, Mr. Washkansky!

THE SCIENCE BEHIND IT

MANY YEARS AGO, PEOPLE BELIEVED THAT THE heart was not just an important part of the body but also the guide to someone's personality—and maybe even the soul. About 500 years ago, scientists began to understand its true role as the powerhouse of the body's blood flow. This understanding removed a lot of the mystery and made it easier to think of the heart as a muscle with special responsibilities.

Organ transplants remained a dream for centuries. Dramatic advances in the late 18th through the early 20th centuries, though, made transplanting organs seem like a possibility. Still, doctors recognized that one of the biggest problems was rejection—the patient's body would think that the new organ was an invader that had to be destroyed. In order for transplants to work, this problem would need to be solved.

By the early 20th century, doctors were providing blood transfusions—giving a patient someone else's healthy blood—with mixed results. Sometimes the blood seemed to be rejected, and other times it wasn't. Then Austrian Karl Landsteiner discovered that people had different types of blood (called blood groups). The differences have to do with the grouping of proteins—antigens and antibodies—which are on the front line in the body's battle against "invaders." People with identical blood groups could use each other's blood freely in a transfusion; the risk of rejection rose when incompatible blood groups were mixed.

By the 1950s, surgeons found ways of suturing (sewing during and after an operation) that were quick and effective. Likewise, they had better facilities for storing organs—to be used at very short notice. Dr. Barnard made use of all these advantages in his landmark transplant in 1967. The surgery was a success;it was an infection that killed Washkansky.

Luckily, dramatic advances since 1967 have led to drugs that overcome "rejection" while allowing the body's natural defenses to attack genuine invaders.

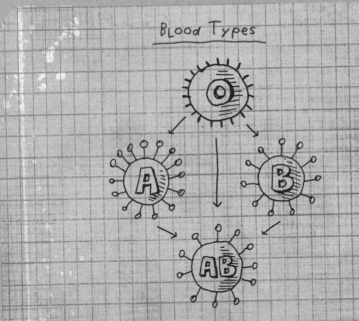

Blood Types

There are four different blood groups: type O, type A, type B, and type AB. If you have blood type AB, you can receive blood from any other blood type. If you have blood types A or B, you can receive blood from only your blood type and type O. If you have blood type O, you can receive from only your own blood type, but you can donate to everybody.

Barnard's Homemade Stethoscope
EXPERIMENT 47

"I hear a beat . . . how sweet." *The Wizard of Oz* Tin Man sings those words in the song "If I Only Had a Heart." The following experiment gives you a chance to hear your heart beating by showing you how to make your own stethoscope (the device doctors and nurses use to listen to your heart and lungs).

MATERIALS

- FLEXIBLE PLASTIC TUBING 1/2 INCH IN DIAMETER AND ABOUT 2 FEET LONG (YOU CAN USUALLY FIND THIS IN A HARDWARE STORE)
- PLASTIC FUNNEL
- TAPE (OPTIONAL)

TAKE CARE!

Never insert any object too far into your ear!

1 Slide the plastic tubing into the narrow end of the funnel. If you can't get a snug fit, then use some tape to secure it.

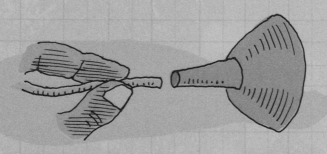

2 Press the wide end of the funnel onto the center of your chest (which is above your heart). Put the other end of the tubing gently into your ear (like a headphone).

3 Count how many heartbeats you hear in 30 seconds. Write it down. Then put the stethoscope down.

4 Run in place as fast as you can for a full minute.

5 Listen to your heart again with the stethoscope. It should sound louder and faster.

Barnard's Heartbeat
EXPERIMENT 48

Getting to understand exactly what the heart is and what it does was the first step in a long medical journey that led to the first successful heart transplant. You can learn a lot, too, by getting some firsthand evidence of how your heart works.

This experiment is a simple and cool way of checking up on your own heart as you see it shaking a straw that is above your chest. You can use its shaking to time your heart rate after a number of activities.

MATERIALS

- MODELING CLAY
- DRINKING STRAWS
- STOPWATCH OR WATCH WITH SECOND HAND
- PAPER
- PEN
- COUCH OR BED

Takes a Lickin' and keeps on Tickin'!

TAKE CARE!

Make sure you find the spot on your neck where you can feel the pulse most strongly. Otherwise, one of the best bits of the experiment—watching the straw "bounce" in time with your heart—won't work as well.

1 The first step is to find your pulse (a place on your body where the heart rate is noticeable): Put two fingers together and feel around the front and side of your neck.

2 The "thump, thump" that you eventually find is your pulse. Remember where it is.

3 Soften up a piece of clay.

4 Lie back on a couch or bed and press the clay onto the pulse area of your neck.

5 Now stick a straw into the clay so that it juts upward. (You should see it vibrating in time with your pulse/heart rate.)

6 Get ready to time it and then count how many times it vibrates in 30 seconds. Then double that number to calculate your heart rate (beats per minute).

7 Write that number on the piece of paper and label it "Resting."

8 Take the clay and straw off and run in place for a minute. Then repeat steps 4, 5, and 6, and label the second number "Running in place."

9 Try to find other activities you can do and then take your pulse. Can you see a connection?

Dieter Issler's
AVALANCHE

HUNKERED DOWN IN THE CAUSE OF SCIENCE

The village of Galtür lies high in the Austrian Alps, near the border with Switzerland. Visitors enjoy hiking in the Alpine meadows and mountain trails in the summer and skiing in the winter. The village itself nestles in a valley at the foot of those mountains.

On February 23, 1999, at the height of the ski season, the peaceful atmosphere of the village was shattered in a matter of minutes. At one minute past four in the afternoon, while skiers were planning their last runs and cafés were full of people enjoying pastries and coffee, disaster struck. A giant slab of snow at the top of the mountain came loose and began sliding downhill. It was what mountain villagers around the world dread—an avalanche.

The avalanche picked up speed as well as new snow as it hurtled down. By the time it reached the village, it was traveling at more than 180 mph and was more than 300 feet high. This terrifying wall of snow, weighing 170,000 tons, took less than a minute to reach the village. It buried or destroyed buildings, making it difficult for rescue teams to reach those who had been in the path of the avalanche. When the village was finally cleared, 31 bodies were removed from the snowy grave.

The Austrian government immediately set up an investigation to find out what had triggered the avalanche (in an area long considered safe) and how future avalanches could be prevented. The investigators could see the damage, but what could be done to avert future tragedies was still a mystery. What they needed was scientific evidence collected *while* an avalanche was in full flow, ideally from inside it.

By a strange coincidence, Dieter Issler of the Swiss Snow and Avalanche Institute had conducted such an experiment in neighboring Switzerland just weeks before the Galtür disaster. Issler's team was based in a concrete bunker at the foot of a steep mountain. Sensitive scientific equipment, including radar, would monitor an avalanche triggered by a dynamite explosion on the mountaintop.

Steel fences are put up to control avalanches in the Swiss Alps.

The scientists survived the avalanche, digging their way out of more than six feet of tightly packed snow. They shared their findings with the investigators and residents of Galtür, where snow fences and other safety features now protect people in the valley.

THE SCIENCE BEHIND IT

IT IS HARD FOR MANY OF US TO UNDERSTAND THAT snow can be a killer, even a mountain of it. But that is because we usually think of being "buried in snow" as something that's part of a snowball fight or other harmless play. However, anyone who has ever experienced an avalanche can set the record straight: Snow can lie at the heart of one of the most sudden and deadly of all natural disasters.

Like landslides and rockslides, avalanches are all about a flow of material traveling very quickly downhill. And although avalanches can scoop up rocks, trees, and even houses along the way, they always begin with snow. The Galtür disaster of 1999 shows that avalanches can gain speeds well above 100 mph: If something carrying hundreds of thousands of tons of snow and debris reaches those speeds, then nearly anything in its path will be knocked down.

People living in mountain valleys have been aware of avalanches for centuries but being aware of and being completely protected against are two different things. Part of the problem is that mountain valleys are always at risk and the only real way of escaping that risk is not to live there. That is impossible to demand of people, so local governments must do their best to minimize the risks.

And that is where the second problem arises. No two avalanches behave in exactly the same way. They depend on factors such as how much and what type of snow lies at the base; how cold the weather is and how much it warms or chills; how steep the slope is;

and which way the wind is blowing. These change-able factors are called "variables."

And that was where the research carried out by the Swiss Snow and Avalanche Institute was so useful. In addition to the daring exploits of Dieter Issler and his fellow scientists "hunkered down" in the bunker to study the avalanche, the Institute had studied the changing weather conditions in the weeks leading up to the Galtür avalanche. Combining the results of the "bunker avalanche" with those of the February 23 disaster enabled the people of Galtür to rebuild their houses using a network of snow fences and other defenses to protect against deadly avalanches.

In avalanche-prone areas, dogs are trained to search out and rescue survivors who might be trapped under feet of snow.

Dieter Issler's Kitchen Avalanche
EXPERIMENT 49

When they're not digging themselves out from two tons of snow, avalanche scientists use scaled-down models to predict the behavior of snow and ice in a wide range of circumstances. This experiment is a version of those models, using household items to take the place of ice, boulders, snow, and rough terrain.

It's best to do this experiment indoors, so that an unexpected gust of wind can't trigger the avalanche before you're ready. You'll be setting up four separate sets of avalanche conditions, arranged as four stripes of the same size across the foam-board base. If you're being really scientific, you'll have a pen and paper handy to identify each type and to record just what happened—and when—to each of those four.

MATERIALS

- PIECE OF FOAM-BOARD (FOAM-CORE) 36 INCHES BY 12 INCHES
- RULER
- PENCIL
- WAX PAPER
- SCISSORS
- BURLAP
- ABOUT 10 JELLY BEANS
- GLUE
- NEWSPAPER
- 2 CUPS GRANULATED SUGAR
- WHITE FLOUR (5-POUND BAG)
- 2 CUPS INSTANT MASHED POTATO FLAKES
- 4 PAPERBACK BOOKS OF THE SAME THICKNESS

TAKE CARE!

Once you've got all four conditions set up, it's really important to conduct the rest of the experiment slowly and steadily. After all, you're looking for what might be very small movements at first, and you want to be able to note just when each of those occurred.

1 Divide the foam core into 4 equal parts. First, measure out and mark dots at 9 inches, 18 inches, and 27 inches along the long sides of the foamboard. Then, use a pencil to connect these dots so that you wind up with four 9 inch wide by 12 inch long panels. It should look like this.

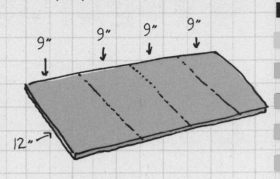

2 Cut a 9-inch by 12-inch strip of wax paper and an identical strip of burlap.

3 Glue 4 jelly beans in a line halfway across (that is, roughly 6 inches down) the lefthand panel (the first on the left) and glue the rest of the jelly beans randomly across the third panel.

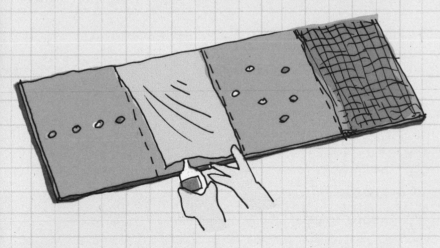

4 Glue the wax paper to the second and the burlap to the fourth panel along.

5 Give the glue time to dry.

6 Spread the newspaper on the table or counter where your avalanche will take place and place the prepared foamboard on it. It should be level at this point, with the prepared side facing up.

7 Shake some granulated sugar over the entire foam-board: This represents the first winter snowfall.

8 Sprinkle half of the flour (representing heavy snowfall) over the entire surface, covering the sugar completely, and pat it all down evenly.

9 Now sprinkle a layer of instant mashed potatoes (representing light dry snow in the coldest part of winter) over everything.

10 Finally, sprinkle the remaining flour (heavy snow in milder, windier conditions) over everything, and pat down evenly.

11 You now have an "avalanche waiting to happen," like Galtür on February 23, 1999.

12 Carefully lift one of the long edges of the foam-board and slide a paperback under it so that you create a slight slope. Observe any slips and other movement.

13 Carefully add more paperbacks one by one to increase the angle slope, noting which conditions are most (and least) stable.

14 With the tip of your pencil, tap lightly at various points on your slope. Can you spot where the most likely place for an avalanche will be?

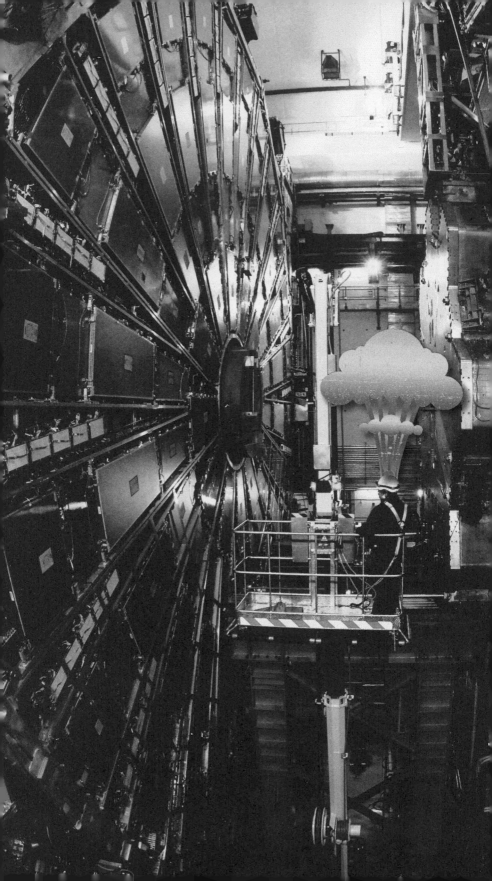

The Large Hadron COLLIDER

THE END OF THE WORLD AS WE KNOW IT?

The best thrillers leave you hanging at the end, not knowing whether the hero will survive or if the evil nasties will have their way. This book is no exception. The 33 chapters up to now have all had happy endings: Either the daring scientist survived the death-defying experiment or the world escaped widespread destruction. This chapter is a little different. Once again, it's about a scientific endeavor that could put us all in mortal danger . . . but we still have to wait for the "see, there was nothing to worry about" conclusion. It could still all go wrong—very wrong!

What's at stake involves learning more about the most distant parts of the universe by exploring the tiniest particles all around us. Over the next 20 years, scientists will use the biggest and most complicated machine ever built to study what happened in the first few instants after the universe was formed. The machine is a particle accelerator called the Large Hadron Collider (LHC) and it lies 300 feet beneath the countryside near the Swiss city of Geneva—the city where Dr. Frankenstein also had his famous lab.

The **Big Bang** is what scientists call the tremendous explosion 15 billion years ago that caused the universe to be created.

Scientists believe that the universe was formed in a huge explosion called the Big Bang, which formed tiny particles that later came together to become planets and stars. The LHC is all about creating some of those very same particles by re-creating—on a microscale—the conditions that existed in the nanosecond immediately following the "Big Bang" explosion (see box). Scientists hope that by doing so, they will be able to answer the most fundamental questions in science about space and time, electromagnetism, gravity, quarks, and the very beginning of the universe. But the scientists face a few problems. Some people believe that by unleashing all that energy, the LHC could bring about the end of the world by creating a black hole that would swallow the Earth in an instant. Talk about potentially catastrophic!

No one really knows what the LHC will ultimately reveal to scientists, or if the

$9 billion cost will have been worth it—but most scientists do believe there's no cause for alarm. Let's keep our fingers crossed.

A **black hole** is a region in space that is so dense that nothing—not even light—can escape it. Although a black hole is invisible, its interaction with other matter can be observed. Astronomers recently discovered evidence of a supermassive black hole in the center of our very own Milky Way Galaxy!

The Globe of Science and Innovation: the birthplace of the Large Hadron Collider.

THE SCIENCE BEHIND IT

THE EUROPEAN COUNCIL FOR NUCLEAR RESEARCH (CERN) the organization behind the Large Hadron Collider, is famous for its ambitious projects, some of which have changed the world. The World Wide Web, for example, was developed in 1989 as a way for CERN scientists to share information with one another. Every time you type a website address using the standard "www" prefix ("World Wide Web"), you're using knowledge and technology developed by CERN. Cool, huh?

The Large Hadron Collider takes its name from hadrons, tiny particles made of even tinier quarks. These hadrons produce even smaller particles when they crash into one another fast enough. The LHC will send two beams of hadrons out in opposite directions, traveling around a 17-mile ring at 99.9999991 percent of the speed of light.

A car traveling at the highest interstate-highway speed limit would take just over two minutes to complete one of the LHC laps. The speeding hadrons will complete 11,245 laps in a second!

These speeds are vital for the LHC to do its job. The other important word in the LHC name is "collider."

CaReFul! I'm tRaveling at almost the speed of Light heRe!

Yeah, well so am I, buddy!

It's not enough to get the hadrons traveling at nearly the speed of light—they've got to collide into each other to work. When two hadrons traveling at these speeds go head to head in this kind of cosmic collision, enormous amounts of energy are involved and something is produced that exists only in theory—a tiny particle called the Higgs boson. This is sometimes called the "God particle" because scientists believe it is responsible for giving all other particles their mass (the material that makes them up). The LHC is expected to provide evidence of the existence of the Higgs boson—or its nonexistence.

It is very difficult getting hadrons to approach the speed of light. The LHC uses more than 9,000 electric magnets to focus the beams. The tunnel must be a vacuum (completely free of matter) and cooled to −459.6 degrees Fahrenheit—colder than outer space. Ten thousand scientists from over one hundred countries have worked tirelessly for years to get the LHC up and running. After a few hiccups getting it operational in 2009, the first big results are expected in 2010. Will it unlock the secrets of the universe? Will it find the "God particle?" Or will it be potentially catastrophic? We'll all soon see.

The Marshmallow Hadron Collider

EXPERIMENT 50

Thinking about the speed of light is enough to give you a headache. Who in the world could possibly measure something traveling at 186,000 miles per *second*? Well, the surprising answer to that is "you."

Using a neat combination of arithmetic, a household appliance, and some yummy marshmallows, you can come to a pretty accurate measurement of the speed of light. It's all about the fact that light (the visible light we see) is just one part of a wider band of radiation, all traveling at the same speed. Microwaves are also part of that band . . . and that's where the marshmallows come in.

The distance between some zapped marshmallows will reveal the wavelength of the microwaves. Remember that we're working in meters, so the centimeter amount measures hundredths of a meter. And a label on the microwave will reveal the frequency (how often those waves vibrate each second). You can then use the calculator to tap in amounts for the following equation:

frequency x wavelength = velocity (or speed)

And remember: You can eat the experiment once you've done all the calculations.

MATERIALS

- **MICROWAVE-SAFE DINNER PLATE**
- **MARSHMALLOWS**
- **MICROWAVE OVEN (WITHOUT A TURNTABLE, OR WITH TURNTABLE REMOVED)**
- **RULER (WITH CENTIMETER MARKS)**
- **CALCULATOR**

TAKE CARE!

Don't get worried about the centimeters and meters if you're unfamiliar with them. If the amount you measure in step 4 is, say, 6 centimeters and you double it to get the wavelength, then you can write 12 centimeters in your calculation as 0.12.